ALL THE DIFFERENCE SERIES

Luke's Curious Christmas

Whatever Happened to Manhood?
A Return to Biblical Manhood

Whatever Happened to Manhood?
A Return to Biblical Manhood Study Guide

Forthcoming:

Your Work Matters

In the Name of Love

The Power of a Merry Heart

To Nineveh—Going Overboard for a
Lost Generation

REPORTING THE FIRST *Advent*

LUKE'S CURIOUS *Christmas*

By WAYNE BRAUDRICK

LAMPION Press

Silverton, OR

Lampion Press, LLC
P. O. Box 932
Silverton, OR 97381

ISBN: 978-1-942614-09-8

Library of Congress Control Number: 2015954898

Formatting and cover design by Amy Cole, JPL Design Solutions

Printed in the United States of America

TO JANNA

WHO LOVES JESUS, CHRISTMAS, AND ME

CONTENTS

FOREWORD

In my country, Uganda, Christmas means a time for the rare opportunity for many to eat some meat and to get a new dress. Marriages are known to break up, because the husband did not buy a new dress for the wife.

On Christmas Day, churches are full and overflowing, because everybody goes to church, even those who are not church-goers. It is a social event, with people adorning their new clothes.

In Uganda, Christmas is generally a social event. It is not about Christ, the Saviour!

When I came to America with my family in November 1984 to study at Dallas Theological Seminary, things were not any different, except it was on a much, much larger scale—the shopping and gift-buying frenzy and all. I was simply blown away. My family and I joined the frenzy.

On Christmas Day, we dressed up and drove to church. Alas! There was nobody at the church! Could the rapture have occurred? No. In America, most people do not go to church on Christmas Day! This remains the most memorable cultural shock I got, when I came to America.

But the thing is, in Uganda, in America and in all countries, the meaning of Christmas needs retrieving. Christmas is simply a social event. It is not about Christ, the Saviour. Christ is in the background. In more and more countries, Christ is not even there at all.

In *Luke's Curious Christmas,* Dr. Braudrick is addressing a real need. And he has done it well, in substance and in method and style. He has focused on some key terms to bring out the meaning of Christmas. He has given us insightful background and atmosphere to give us a feel of that first Christmas. He has used illustrations, stories, songs and poems to help drive the message of Christmas home. His style is engaging, interesting and easy to read.

I highly commend to you Dr. Braudrick's *Luke's Curious Christmas.* May God use it for a fresh impact on today's society regarding the true meaning of Christmas.

Bishop Dr. Michael Kyomya,
Jinja, Uganda

INTRODUCTION

WE NEED A LOT OF CHRISTMAS

We don't need a little Christmas. We need *a lot* of Christmas! We need Christmas in all its depth and glory. We need the joy, peace, and humility that are far too often absent from the season and celebrations of it. We need to find a way for the stuff of earth to stop crowding out our focus on God's revelation at Christmas. We need to go straight to the heart of Christmas such that we accept the Savior's revelation, joy, peace, and humility; and then delight in making Him known.

The only way to get to that heart of Christmas is through God's Word. Another party, television special, or fad diet will achieve nothing toward our real need. Neither will Grinch-inspired isolation or Crankish refusal to spend money on others. The Gospel of Luke was written to expressly meet our need. In some of the most brilliant literature ever penned, Luke grants us an amazingly fresh understanding of exactly what Christmas is about and how it changes our lives.

LUKE'S AMAZING ACHIEVEMENT

Luke, the author of the gospel that bears his name, uses some very curious terminology in his Christmas account—especially in describing the night of the Savior's birth. These interesting, specific, and rare word plays are dynamic. They are key to our understanding of Christmas because they expose the depth of reality God is trying to communicate to people. About a century ago A. T. Robertson, one of the great Greek scholars of the New Testament, summarized the result:

> Luke handles the data acquired with care and skill ... The outcome is what [Ernest] Renan called the most beautiful book in the world. Literary charm is here beyond dispute. It is a book that only a man with genuine culture and literary genius could write ... There is a delicate finish of detail and proportion of parts that give the balance and poise that come only from a full knowledge of the subject, the chief element in a good style ... This scientific physician, this man of the schools, this converted Gentile, this devoted friend of Paul, comes to the study of the life of Christ with a trained intellect, with an historian's method of research, with a physician's care in diagnosis and discrimination, with a charm and style all his own, with reverence for and loyalty to Jesus Christ as Lord and Savior.[1]

Hopefully Luke's account and words will enrich your understanding of the greatest birth in history!

A LITTLE BIT OF BACKGROUND

Before we dive into Luke's curious Christmas terminology, there are a few critical textual issues that bear particularly on the passage where we will camp—Luke chapter 2. These issues can be grouped as historical, stylistic, and grammatical in nature. (Some of this material will be covered in the chapters, but it seems helpful to gather it together here as an easily-accessible introduction to Luke, his time, and his style.)

1. History

The nineteenth century was quite unkind to Luke. He was the favorite whipping boy of the German "higher" critics of New Testament studies who claimed the text to be the most historically inaccurate work of all time. The impact of this slanted and assumptive onslaught was so

1 A. T. Robertson, *Word Pictures in the New Testament.* Vol. II *Luke* (Nashville: B&H Books, 1973), xiii.

powerful that even evangelicals diminished their use of the book. Some even refrained from preaching and teaching Luke at all. Thankfully, the twentieth century brought a powerful reversal. Archaeology was predominantly responsible for Luke's re-elevation, as find after find demanded a framework that supported Luke's validity. With the finding of the Pontius Pilate stone in Caesarea, Luke's critics were at last forced to capitulate. Even early in the twentieth century Sir William Ramsey noted in his *Bearing of Recent Discovery on the Trustworthiness of the New Testament*, "So many items, where Luke once stood alone, have been confirmed by recent discoveries that the burden of proof now rests on those who challenge Luke."[2] Today, dating discussions continue, but they do so on a more rational footing. We are wise to use Luke as an authoritative guide for understanding Christmas.

2. Style

Luke was a physician, and he writes like one—a truth that needs a bit of explanation for a modern audience. Through the influence of Aristotle and Ptolemy and via the free market of learning in the first century, physicians were well-educated and becoming more "scientific." However, we mustn't think of them like a modern scientifically-trained doctor. Medicine was still centered on the cult of Asclepius and a-religious medicine would have made no sense to a physician of that era. This has bearing on our text in that Luke teaches us how to scientifically approach a supernatural Lord. Luke, completely content with the reality of miracles, is a trained observer who relates miraculous happenings as true because they are. While refusing to dabble in non-scientific superstition, he does not feel the modern embarrassment that tries to explain away the miraculous.

3. Vocabulary

Luke is rather like Shakespeare. He tells a story that is simply grasped yet demands a great deal from the reader who wants to dig deeper. For example, Luke's Greek draws from a wide array of authors, lifting terms of great import and specific meaning and then placing those terms in

2 Sir William Mitchell Ramsay, *The Bearing of Recent Discovery on the Trustworthiness of the New Testament* (London: Hodder and Staughton, 1915), 47.

his gospel. Guided of the Holy Spirit, Luke invites us to gain even more understanding about the Christ through mining these terms. Further, Luke uses Hebrew, with which he has more than mere passing knowledge. We are uncertain how Luke gained his skill with Hebrew, though speculations range from reading the Septuagint (the Greek translation of the Hebrew Scriptures) to his time spent with the Apostle Paul. Luke's sense of humor is wonderfully transcultural, but is especially founded on the Hebrew love of the unexpected. He also uses special Hebraisms that deepen the text and display his capacity with that tongue.

Of course, Luke is a Gentile and is writing for a Gentile audience. That is clear in his facility with Greek. In fact, this remarkable man was obviously well-read as he borrows words from ancient Greek authors writing in what we call "Classical Greek" while also taking terms from his contemporaries using a different form of Greek termed *Koine* ("common"). Many of these are rare terms appearing nowhere else in Scripture. Some are compound words formed by Luke. He brilliantly crafted these unique words to be accessible to his audience while giving great specificity about his subject. These special terms will be the heart of our Advent study.

CHAPTER ONE

THE JOY AND PEACE OF CHRISTMAS

CHAPTER SUMMARY: The joy of Christmas is the good news that God has reached toward people. The peace is a deep calming that comes from thinking on the truth that God brings peace to us in Jesus.
LIFE CHANGE OBJECTIVE: That we find joyful peace in Jesus.

IMAGINE YOU ARE A GUARD ON DUTY AT A LITTLE FORT. Further, suppose that you are on guard duty because your small kingdom is in rebellion against the mighty Emperor. Your people have refused to pay any taxes because the Emperor's taxes were beyond your ability to pay. So, your little nation just settled into a kind of passive aggression, taking solace in your location far away from the Emperor. You're expectantly hopeful that he won't even mess with your little world, anyway. But people still draw guard duty, just in case.

It's late at night. You're just sitting at your post … got the picture? When suddenly flares go off all around and everything is lit up. And in that light, you see a massive army is gathering all around you. Thousands upon thousands of soldiers suddenly appear, voicing a marching chant in unison. It's awesome! And horrifying, because you are sure why they have come: to judge and enslave you and your people. Then, the mouthpiece of the Emperor steps up and to you, the little guard at the gate, he says:

> Peace. We have come to tell you that your taxes will be paid in full by another. You have the Emperor's love.

Doesn't that sound like something from a Monty Python skit? Who uses a mighty army to bring a message of peace? It's ironic to the point of hilarity! Armies are for killing and breaking; they are not a messenger service. Who uses a giant army to bring a peace message? God does.

Look at the remarkable true story in Luke 2:

> In the same region, shepherds were staying out in the fields and keeping watch at night over their flock. Then an angel of the Lord stood before them, and the glory of the Lord shone around them, and they were terrified. But the angel said to them, "Don't be afraid, for look, I proclaim to you good news of great joy that will be for all the people: Today a Savior, who is Messiah the Lord, was born for you in the city of David. This will be the sign for you: You will find a baby wrapped snugly in cloth and lying in a feeding trough."
>
> Suddenly there was a multitude of the heavenly host with the angel, praising God and saying:
>
> Glory to God in the highest heaven,
> and peace on earth to people He favors! (Luke 2:18-14 HCSB)

Here's is God's holy Word about Christmas, delivered through the human author, Luke. And Luke enjoys exposing the unexpected, marvelous humor of God. God has a formidable heavenly army appear and, in a wild twist, they come to bring a message of peace.

THE AUTHOR

Before we dive further into this passage, let's discuss a bit about the human author. Luke is an extremely bright, well-educated Gentile. That is clear in his ability with languages. In fact, this remarkable man was obviously well-read as he borrows words from both kinds of Greek—classical and *Koine.* Many of Luke's words are rare terms appearing nowhere else in scripture. Some are compound words formed by Luke to be accessible to his audience but unique nonetheless. By the way, Luke was so well-educated that he learned and uses Hebrew, showing a more than a passing knowledge of the Old Testament. So it's likely safe to say that Luke was a smarter, better writer than many alive today.

> We also know Luke is a physician, as the Apostle Paul tells us in his letter to Colossae:
>
> Luke the beloved physician greets you, as does Demas. (Colossians 4:14 ESV)

Luke understandably uses words appearing in Greek medical texts of his time; words that do not appear elsewhere in the Bible. Luke also goes out of his way to describe the illnesses of those who come to Jesus for healing. In other words, Luke writes like a doctor—meaning his handwriting is illegible. Seriously, first-century medicine requires a bit of explanation for us as a modern audience.

In the first century, physicians were well-educated and becoming more "scientific." However, we mustn't think of them like a modern scientifically trained doctor. Medicine was still centered on the cult of Asclepius and a-religious medicine would have made no sense to a first-century physician. This has bearing on our text in that Luke teaches us how to scientifically approach a supernatural Lord.

Luke, completely content with the reality of miracles, is a trained observer who relates miraculous happenings as true because they are. He does not feel the modern embarrassment that tries to explain away the miraculous. However, neither does Luke dabble in superstition. Luke's education does not drive him away from belief in Jesus. Rather, Luke the physician grasps both the scientific reality and the supernatural truth of Jesus. Luke fell in love with the real Jesus, who is both supernatural and rational.

And Luke's love for Jesus is what causes him to become a ministry partner with Paul. Paul, the Jewish Apostle to the Gentiles, ended up leaning very heavily on this well-educated Gentile doctor. Luke was the official recorder of the work of the early churches, especially the early mission trips that spread the gospel of Jesus.

Luke joined Paul on the second great missionary journey, and was the only friend to remain true to Paul through all his trials. Even Demas, the guy we saw mentioned earlier with Luke, deserted Paul. However, Luke was a faithful partner to the end. It was Luke who put down on paper the gospel Paul taught so well. We call that the record *The Gospel of Luke*. Later, the Holy Spirit moved Luke to write of the mission trips and early churches—that's the book we call *Acts* or *the Acts of the Apostles*.

THE WRITING

Luke is somewhat like Shakespeare. They each tell a story that is simply grasped yet demands a great deal from the reader who wants to dig deeper. Each of these literary masters writes clear and strong plots. They have bold characters, dramatic scenes, and memorable lines. Most people reflexively know Hamlet's immortal line: "To be, or not to be … " While Luke gave us the magnificent words spoken in a million Christmas pageants, "Do not be afraid, for behold … "

Luke is one of the greatest authors of all time, and not just because the Holy Spirit wrote His scripture through Luke. Luke's own wit, wisdom and word choices jump out, showing how God blessed him as a phenomenal writer. Luke is not just memorable. He's deep. Again, Shakespeare is the rare author who is similar, though in my opinion Shakespeare cannot match Luke's depth.

This kind of writer has wheels within wheels—deeper plots going on inside the story. Just as *Romeo and Juliet* is more than a love story, Jesus isn't just healing physical illnesses in Luke's account. There's more going on. The characters are really alive and fully developed. As just one example, Luke gives us the fullest picture of how Jesus was rejected on so many different levels by so many different people.

Finally, Luke pulls off the amazing feat of crafting pithy, simple writing that a child can understand. Yet, at the same time his text demands that we look more deeply into individual words. Even more than the actions, it is the verbiage that drives the meaning in Luke's Gospel. That's why we are studying some curious words of Luke's—to go deeper than the surface level of Christmas. These interesting, specific, and rare word plays are dynamic. They are also key to our understanding of Christmas because they expose the depth of reality God is trying to communicate to people. If you want to know what Christmas is all about, Charlie Brown, you need Luke's words.

THE WIT

Another thing should be understood about Luke's writing: he is funny! His sense of humor is founded on his love of the unexpected and his knowledge of different cultures. That combination—love of the unexpected and knowledge of different languages—reminds me of a favorite commercial sent to me by a friend in Germany. It opens with a crusty old veteran of the German Coast Guard showing the new recruit the ropes. Speaking in a torrent of German, he points out the various equipment, slaps the new kid on the shoulder, and leaves. A few seconds later, the radio crackles to life as a British voice says, "Mayday! Mayday! Hello, Can you hear us? We are sinking!" To which the young German man replies in heavily-accented English, "Hello. Zis is zee German Coast Guart." The British captain repeats, "We are sinking! Mayday! We are sinking!" And the German replies, "What are you sinking [thinking] about?" Immediately, Beethoven's "Ode to Joy" plays while the Berlitz company touts their classes to learn English.[3]

"What are you sinking about?" That's funny! And so is Luke. He plays with different languages just like that. For example, Luke starts his whole gospel with the story of Zacharias in the Temple. There are great cultural jokes here. Zacharias the priest doesn't believe Gabriel the angel when Gabriel says that Zacharias is going to have a son. Therefore, Gabriel makes Zacharias mute until the boy John is born.

3 "German Coastguard Sinking - Learn English Commercial." *YouTube*. YouTube, n.d. Web. 17 June 2015.

Now, Zacharias was ministering inside the holy place of the Temple at the time. Moses' Law and Jewish culture reveal why that's so funny. According to the Law, if God rejects the people's sacrifice the priest could get killed in the holy place. So when Zacharias doesn't answer them, Luke records how the people outside got nervous. Yeah, I bet they did!

I marvel at the depth of this humor. God did reject their sacrifice. Even in his humor, Luke is thinking here. They could never sacrifice enough to please God. So God sent this boy to Zacharias—a boy called John the Baptizer—to make a way for God's own sacrifice. God was sending his own Son to be the sacrifice, because He loved people who don't deserve His love. Even while chuckling over the miscommunication (or, rather, non-communication) between the priest and the people, Luke is dealing with a majestic and serious subject.

LUKE'S CURIOUS CHRISTMAS WORDS TEACH US A GREAT DEAL ABOUT THE JOY OF CHRISTMAS.

Now that we know more about the author, let's learn from what he says to us. Consider verse 10 again.

> But the angel said to them, "Don't be afraid, for look, I proclaim to you good news of great joy that will be for all the people (Luke 2:10 HCSB)

The story is familiar, but the words chosen are very interesting. And Luke's curious Christmas words teach us a great deal about the joy of Christmas. Here in verse 10, Luke gives us a very strange transliterated phrase that is singular in all literature: *humin evangelizomai megalen charan* [ὑμῖν εὐαγγελίζομαι μεγάλην χαρὰν].

The Holman Bible translation quoted above translates this, "I proclaim to you good news of great joy." John Wycliffe, the wonderful early translator of the Bible into English rendered the clause, "I evangelize to you a great joy!" I would put it, "I evangelize to you awesome, gracious, joy!"

This is an intriguing turn of phrase. See the word "*evangelizomai*?" That verb is borrowed from the Greek playwright Aristophanes, who wrote almost 500 years before Luke wrote. In Luke's day, no one talked in old-fashioned words like that. But Luke did, and did so for a reason. We can feel the stiltedness even in our language today. We don't say things like, "I evangelize to you." The Greeks to whom Luke wrote didn't talk like that either.

God is having Luke record the angel's words in a very specific way for very important reasons. It's done to teach some significant lessons:

1. Christmas represents good news.
2. Christmas comes from God to humans.
3. Christmas represents mega-joy—a deep, peaceful kind of joy.

CHRISTMAS REPRESENTS GOOD NEWS.

Think about the greatest surprise present you ever received. I have been blessed with many, though few could match the new bike on Christmas when I was six years old. Such surprises are so moving and fun! And that is the spirit of the word *evangelizomai*. Christmas represents fun, good news.

Ev is the root word of *evangelizomai*. It means "good." Luke likes what Aristophanes did. He combined *ev* with *aggelos*. *Aggelos* means "to bring a word or a message." (We get the word "angel" from *aggelos,* because angels are God's messengers.) The Greek playwright had combined these into a verb that meant "I bring good news."

Why does Luke utilize this odd and old construction? Because God guided him to this unique way of relating the most important news ever shared. The Emperor of the universe has appeared in the night, unexpectedly. And he humbly comes to share our sufferings. He comes to lodge with us, abide with us, and ultimately to pay all the price of our sins. That is the most surprising, best news of all time. Though no one word could capture the majesty, surprise, and joy of that message, a really august term seems appropriate. Christmas is the grandest news ever, and as such is worthy of a stately word.

CHRISTMAS COMES FROM GOD TO HUMANS.

Look at the second lesson contained in verse 10's words: God is coming to rescue people. That's the real joy of Christmas—God has reached toward people. He has condescended to our level in order to bless us.

Think back to when you were a child. When a big grown-up person spoke with you, did you prefer they tower over you standing very tall? Or did you prefer when they bent down and spoke to you eye-to-eye. Every child I know (and they are a legion that richly bless my life) prefers the latter. They don't presume that lowering completely reduces the adult to child status, but they appreciate the effort to connect at a kid level.

With that in mind, consider what God did in bringing Jesus to us. He descended to us. This is so important. The angel says that he brings the news to people … not the other way around.

In the lead up to Christmas, we are going to see lots of movies talking about good people should be and how if we can be good, we'll bring good news to God. Now of course, God loves for us to be righteous. But it doesn't start with us! The Bible is completely clear in declaring that our righteousness is filthy rags. (See Isaiah 64:6.) We need God to come to us. We have nothing to offer Him on our own. We need His righteousness that comes through our faith in Jesus.

To emphasize this concept, a friend recommended we read these verses:

> You have given me the shield of Your salvation;
>
> Your right hand upholds me,
> and Your humility exalts me. (Psalm 18:35 HCSB)
>
> Who is like the Lord our God,
>
> Who is enthroned on high,
> Who humbles Himself to behold
> *The things that are* in heaven and in the earth?
> He raises the poor from the dust
> And lifts the needy from the ash heap,
> To make *them* sit with princes,
>
> With the princes of His people. (Psalm 113:5-8 NASB)

The point is obvious. Christmas comes from God who reaches down to humans.

CHRISTMAS REPRESENTS MEGA-JOY.

Now, you may have recognized a part of Luke's verbiage, because it's a term we still use today. See the "mega" in there? *Megalen* means super-sized, not so much in size as in power. It means awesome or great. *Charan* means a deep, peaceful kind of delight. *Charan* is joy. Put together, Luke shows us God bringing humans a deep, powerful kind of joy. This is something new that wells up from inside because the delight of God coming to us is too powerful … too mega … too awesome to be contained. It's a bubbling up joy that is rich and mighty. And it changes the world.

In August 2006, the yacht *Maiken* was traveling near the Togo archipelago in the South Pacific when they saw what looked like sand floating on top of the water. It turned out to be what is called a pumice raft—volcanic stones spewed out by an active volcano. But the *Maiken* was way out in the middle of blue water. There was no land in sight, with or without a volcano. The pumice raft became so thick, it actually slowed the ship from 7 knots down to 1 knot of speed.

Then, off in the distance the crew spied a plume of black ash rising from the sea. Over the next hour they experienced something very rare. They witnessed the birth of a brand new island bubbling up from beneath the sea. [Using the keywords "Yacht Maiken," you can look it up online and enjoy their amazing photographs of the phenomenon.] That is *megalen charan*. That is Christmas. Mega-joy that bubbles up and changes the world.

LUKE'S CURIOUS CHRISTMAS WORDS CONTINUE WITH INSTRUCTION ABOUT PEACE.

Let's think a bit more on verse 14:

> Glory to God in the highest heaven,
> and peace on earth to people He favors! (Luke 2:14 HCSB)

Luke here gives us *eirene en anthropois eudokias* [εἰρήνη ἐν ἀνθρώποις εὐδοκίας]—what we render "peace on earth [or "earth's humans"] with whom He is pleased [or "whom He favors"]." This is a shocking phrase in Luke's Greek. This was an in-your-face, radical statement that would never have appeared in any pagan Greek text. This phrase is exclusively Christian. Luke's construction makes sense to no other worldview. You see, no other world religion believes that God and humans are distinct and can yet be joined together in peaceful relationship.

The pagans believed in gods totally separate. They never offered peace toward humans. Luke's idea would have been absurd to them. Even today, world religions fall into two big categories:

1. Humans are condemned because God has not offered peace. These folks always have rules people must keep to try and work their way to salvific peace with God.
2. Humans have a kind of peace because they offer it to themselves. How can they do that? Each person is his own god and can offer peace to himself. These folks spend a lot of time meditating on peace "within" themselves or entertaining themselves.

Luke's idea rejects that dichotomy and is thus completely novel. There is a real holy God. He is not us. Yet He alone offers real and lasting peace to humans. *Eirene en anthropois eudokias* is a world-changing idea. It's so wild that various English translations struggle with how to effectively render the concept into our tongue. Though I'm no Greek scholar, it seems to me that Dr. Robertson's translation is best: "joined peace toward good-thinking people."[4]

PEACE IS FOUND IN UNITY WITH GOD.

The more we examine the Greek text, the richer we find Luke's declaration. For example, the root word of *eirene*, *eiro,* originally meant to "join." Later, *eirene* carried the idea of "peace" because that which is joined together is no longer at odds with each other. Therefore, when Luke says *eirene*, he is telling us that God has declared an opportunity for humans to be joined in peace with God. No longer at odds, humans can live in harmony with the Almighty.

Again, please notice that this peace comes top-down, not bottom-up. It is God who declares peace, not mankind. Peace comes from God

4 A. T. Robertson, *Word Pictures in the New Testament.* Vol. II *Luke* (Nashville, TN: B&H Books, 1973), 13.

to man as a result of relationship, not from man earning his way to God. That *en*, the little preposition, is really important in the phrase *eirene en anthropois eudokias*. It means "toward" and shows that real peace doesn't come from us reaching toward God. Luke's curious Christmas teaches us that God moves peace toward us.

This is completely unexpected, unprecedented, and precious. God has given us peace, by joining people to Himself. He has adopted us into His family. (By the way, adoption becomes a favorite image of Paul and Luke.) We are no longer aliens separated from God. By His grace alone we are grafted in, joined, and have peace. A friend and I were discussing this and he compared it to a story he heard that revolves around the age-old animosity between squirrels and dogs. Here's what he wrote:

> A lady near here [My friend lives in Seattle.] named Debbie found a baby squirrel abandoned near her home. Debbie named the baby squirrel Finnegan and took him in. Her biggest concern in bringing in the needy orphan was some anticipated antagonism from her little Papillion dog named Madame Giselle. Amazingly, Madame Giselle condescended to accept the needy Finnegan, putting Debbie at ease. Yet she never expected what happened next. Madame Giselle gave birth not long after Finnegan's arrival, and Finnegan was just joined right in to the family. Our paper even had a photo of little Finnegan feeding along with Madame Giselle's pups.[5]

That, friends, is what Luke was saying in writing that shocking word *eirene*. Peace.

PEACE ARRIVES BY THINKING THROUGH THE TRUTHS OF JESUS.

Peace is found in unity with God. And peace arrives by thinking through the truths of Jesus. That's the story from this final word of our Greek phrase—*eudokias*. It's a combination of the words for "good" and "thinking." It was used as a kind of shorthand term for favor or pleasure, but

5 Private correspondence with author. You can see the mentioned photo and more at http://snopes.com/photos/animals/finnegan.asp.

it retained the idea of right reasoning. *Eudokias* is pleasure that comes from right thinking. Luke seems to be saying that God is pleased with those who think things through. They are the ones for whom peace is actuated.

The holiday season, with its manifold opportunities for people watching, illustrates Luke's point. Study all the holiday mess swirling around you this year and you'll notice one great theme: the people who think on Jesus have peace even in the maelstrom. Those concerned with other things do not.

Most of the world is caught up in stinking thinking. Some people are even actively trying to think about nothing, a nonsensical proposition that sometimes succeeds, bringing the person exactly what they sought—nothing. Then that nothing is falsely called peace. Others humans are full of selfish or silly thoughts, determined to think about anything but the truth. Saccharine silliness is all they have, so they pretend it's the meaningful peace their soul desperately needs.

God instead offers real peace. It comes through good, hard thinking. The truth is that Jesus is real. He is proven to be the Son of God, the Savior Messiah who entered time and space as a little baby born in Bethlehem. He is the one who paid in full our taxes owed to God Almighty, a debt brought on by our sin. Those who think through such things respond to Jesus, and as a result they receive real peace.

The joy of Christmas is the good news that God has reached toward people. The peace of Christmas is a deep calming that comes from thinking on the truth that God brings peace to us in Jesus. I encourage you to stop for a few minutes and meditate on that right now. Biblical meditation is *eudokias*—thinking on something that is true—so think for a minute about Jesus and the joy and peace of Christmas.

It Came Upon a Midnight Clear
(Edmund Sears[6])

It came upon the midnight clear,
That glorious song of old,
From angels bending near the earth,
To touch their harps of gold:

6 Edmund Sears, 1849. Public domain.

"Peace on the earth, goodwill to men,
From heaven's all-gracious King."
The world in solemn stillness lay,
To hear the angels sing.

Still through the cloven skies they come,
With peaceful wings unfurled,
And still their heavenly music floats
O'er all the weary world;
Above its sad and lowly plains,
They bend on hovering wing,
And ever o'er its Babel sounds
The blessèd angels sing.

And ye, beneath life's crushing load,
Whose forms are bending low,
Who toil along the climbing way
With painful steps and slow,
Look now! for glad and golden hours
come swiftly on the wing.
O rest beside the weary road,
And hear the angels sing!

For lo!, the days are hastening on,
By prophet bards foretold,
When with the ever-circling years
Comes round the age of gold
When peace shall over all the earth
Its ancient splendors fling,
And the whole world give back the song
Which now the angels sing.

CHAPTER 2

THE HUMILITY OF CHRISTMAS

CHAPTER SUMMARY: Luke is the only one to record the story regarding the temporary homeless status of Joseph, Mary, and Jesus. He likewise singularly points out the details of the manger and swaddling clothes. This emphasizes humility as an attribute of God, coupling that powerful and surprising truth with God's humor, timing, and sacrifice.
LIFE CHANGE OBJECTIVE: That we imitate Jesus and witness to His love.

PHENOMENAL COSMIC POWER ... ITTY-BITTY LIVING SPACE

You are likely familiar with the movie *Aladdin.* When the film was released, *Aladdin* became the runaway hit of that Christmas box office season. And the main reason was the genie character—brilliantly drawn by Eric Goldberg and hilariously voiced by Robin Williams. People flocked to the movie mainly because the genie was so funny. I enjoyed the movie; in fact, it's one of the few films I've ever paid to see twice at the theatre.

I loved the humor, but what really attracted me were some serious thoughts taking place within the humor. Maybe because I saw the movie at Christmas, I was struck by a powerful parallel between Genie's self-description and the *Gospel of Luke*. In the film, the genie gives a speech that always makes me think of Luke chapter 2. Genie is summarizing what's it's like to be a potent servant here on earth who lives in a tiny lamp. He says, "It's part and parcel of the whole Genie gig: Phenomenal Cosmic Power ... itty, bitty living space." That line struck me as a great representation of Jesus' choice to come as a baby human being. This is remarkable power—God Himself—dwelling with us as a true human. Phenomenal Cosmic Power ... itty, bitty living space. That's the essence of the humility of Christmas, something especially highlighted in Luke's writing. An amazing linguist inspired of the Holy Spirit, Dr. Luke employs some rare and intricate language to get across his message about the humility of Christmas.

For example, reach past what may be familiar and listen to the exquisite cadences of Luke 2:

> Now in those days a decree went out from Caesar Augustus, that a census be taken of all the inhabited earth. This was the first census taken while Quirinius was governor of Syria. And everyone was on his way to register for the census, each to his own city. Joseph also went up from Galilee, from the city of Nazareth, to Judea, to the city of David which is called Bethlehem, because he was of the house and family of David, in order to register along with Mary, who was engaged to him, and was with child. While they were there, the days were completed for her to give birth. And she gave birth to her firstborn son; and she wrapped Him in cloths, and laid Him in a manger, because there was no room for them in the inn. (Luke 2:1-7 NASB)

INHABITED EARTH

This is God's humility. Let's examine some of the specific terms used here, because they have a lot to teach us. Begin with the phrase "inhabited earth" in the first sentence. This is a compound word οἰκουμένην [*oikoumene*] meaning "land that is dwelt on." The experts say that the term is formed by a very complex combination of a common Greek word for occupying a property *oikeo* [οἰκέω] and a primitive word used for habitable land *ge* [γῆ].

This clever combination is a favorite of Luke's. Eight of the 15 appearances of *oikoumene* in the New Testament appear in Luke's writing. Here he obviously intends it as a way to depict the whole Roman Empire; yet, Luke is saying something even more pointed in this verbiage. As you likely know, much of the habitable world was controlled by Rome in the first century. But Rome, under the Caesars, didn't just oversee an area. They occupied it. Controlled it. That word Luke used is the same one used for taking occupation of a house, and the Romans saw the world as their private property.

They took possession of everything. They made all the earth theirs. They called the massive Mediterranean *Mare Nostrum*—Latin for "our sea." And their occupation was especially resented in Israel. In fact, one Latin word can illustrate how harshly the Romans controlled Israel. Look at a historical map and find the name for the province in which the Messiah is born. It's not titled Israel or even Judea. On Roman maps it was called *Palestina*—Palestine. Do you know who created that name? The Romans. They thought it a cruel and funny joke to name the province after Israel's enemies from 1000 years before—the Philistines. Thus, every time a Jew hears a Roman speak about the land, the Jew has the old Philistine name thrown back in his face. Israel is under a harsh Roman yoke, something that "inhabited earth" [*oikoumene*] reveals.

And yet—get this—that's the environment chosen by God for the birth of the Messiah. Would you want to give birth in a place occupied by forces that mock you and take over your home? Of course not! And yet God did. Such is the humility inherent in the Messiah, that God sent him as a baby right in the middle of an ugly occupied zone.

"WRAPPED HIM IN CLOTHS"

For our next word, slide down to the last sentence, verse 7, where Mary "wrapped him in cloths." Today, we wrap our babies in blankets, folding the corners over to "swaddle" the child. (Where I live in Texas, this is often dubbed a "baby burrito.") Such a tight wrap on an infant, especially a newborn, makes him feel safe and secure. Studies have shown that tightly-swaddled babies enjoy REM sleep for much longer than infants merely underneath a blanket.

Luke tells us that Mary took this a step further, following the widespread custom of her time. "Wrapped him in cloths" is one long word in verse 7: *espargarnosen* [ἐσπαργάνωσεν]. This is a special word from Greek medical texts that only Luke uses in the New Testament. The term describes the practice of completely wrapping a newborn up in strips of overlapped cloth. It was tighter and more binding than our baby burrito. It was also a lot more work.

Here's the really cool part. In the Greek translation of the Old Testament, the same word is used. But in the Old Testament, it is *God* doing the swaddling. Look at Job 39:

> "Where were you when I laid the foundation of the earth?
> … When I made a cloud its garment,
>
> And thick darkness its swaddling band [*espargarnosen*]" (Job 39:4,9 NASB)

God says, "Look here. I made the very earth! In particular, I swaddled it with darkness at night so it could rest and sleep." God is all powerful! He is the swaddler. He is the almighty. Colossians 1 reminds us that Jesus was Himself Creator. He, fully God, swaddles the earth with needed darkness. And yet He submitted to being swaddled Himself. That's the humility of Christmas.

Speaking of the humility of Christmas, this story was sent to me by a mother who shall remain protected in anonymity:

> I will never forget my children's Christmas pageant at church.
>
> My daughter was playing Mary, two of my sons were shepherds and my youngest son was a wise man. This was their moment to shine.
>
> My five-year-old shepherd had practiced his line, "We found the babe wrapped in swaddling clothes." But he was nervous and said, "The baby was wrapped in wrinkled clothes."
>
> My four-year-old "Mary" said, "That's not '*wrinkled* clothes,' silly.
>
> A wrestling match broke out between Mary and the shepherd. It was finally stopped by another child playing an angel, who bent her halo and lost her left wing in the melee.
>
> I slouched a little lower in my seat when Mary dropped the doll representing Baby Jesus, and it bounced down the aisle crying, "Mama-mama."
>
> My other son stepped forward wearing a bathrobe and a paper crown, knelt at the manger and announced, "We are the three wise men, and we are bringing gifts of gold, common sense and fur."
>
> The congregation dissolved into laughter, and the pageant got a standing ovation. Our pastor got up, wiping tears of laughter from his eyes and said, "I've never enjoyed a Christmas program as much as this one."
>
> For the rest of my life, I'll never hear the Christmas story without thinking of wrinkled clothes & gold, common sense and fur.[7]

In a similar way, I pray that we never hear the Christmas story without thinking of the humility involved in Luke's language.

7 Private story sent to author.

IN A MANGER

Where did Mary lay the baby down? In a manger. A manger was an animal feeding trough, almost certainly made out of stone, since wood was very rare in Israel/Palestine. Archeology proves that many things we think of as wood were almost always made out of stone in the first century. That's why carpenters also worked as stonemasons and people used the same word for both stone-cutter and carpenter.

Of course, the humble nature of this is obvious. When my oldest son was born, our area hospital was brand new and desperate for business. Each child was born in a beautiful suite. Our meals were brought by attendants in tuxedo outfits wearing white gloves. The baby cribs were warm, beautiful wood structures on wheels. Three nurses attended just my one child.

By contrast, Jesus was laid in a cold stone trough they took from some hoofed animal. Such was the baby crib for God.

IN THE CARAVANSARY

Why was Jesus born where animals fed? Because there was no room for them in the "inn." What Luke describes best fits the typical highway caravansary of the time—two-story structures built around a large courtyard. The humans stayed upstairs with the animal stables beneath. Jesus was birthed down underneath with the transport and sacrifice animals. In contemporary terms, he was born in the parking lot of a Motel 6.

In the first century there was no Hilton. There wasn't even a rendition of the later medieval pilgrim house—structures that resembled our modern youth hostels. In the first century, people were expected to stay with relatives. Though Joseph and Mary may have had extended relatives in the little village of Bethlehem, there just wasn't any room for them there. So, they went to the main road near town and stayed at the caravansary, which was also full. How do we know? Because of Luke's curious word. Luke says specifically that they stayed at a place designed for roadside stopovers. The Greek term is *katalumati* [καταλύματι]. It's a compound whose parts mean "place to break up a journey," and describes a structure later called a caravansary by Arab traders. A caravansary was like a truck stop with a wall around it. Donkey and camel caravans would stop at these in order to protect their cargo from robbers. The animals stayed in the courtyard where they were fed in open arcades underneath the human rooms.

Luke tells us that God chose this moment to deliver His Son: when all the rooms upstairs were full and Jesus had to be born in one of the open arcades. That is humility! God could have brought the Messiah to light in a palace, but He chose to birth Jesus in a truck stop instead. As a friend of mine likes to say, “Most humans conceal our humility well.” By contrast, God reveals His humility here. God shows us that He is humble. And His example encourages people who know Him to reveal our humility a little better.

GOD'S IRONIC HUMOR

Of course, God's choice is incredibly ironic. Humor is a big part of this story. On a macro level we have the big king Augustus in his palace on the Roman Palatine Hill ordering around the little king Jesus born in a manger in an area dubbed “Palestine” by occupiers. Yet in reality, the hand of God is behind it all. Everything will flip, and the King Jesus will occupy all hearts while the empire of Augustus will crumble. Even time will be divided into pre- and post- Jesus. (Even the current penchant to call it C.E. “Common Era” plays into God's sovereign humor because the only thing common about it is the birth of Jesus.)

On a micro level, Luke also lets us in on a really funny wordplay. Remember the phrase “inhabited earth” [*oikoumene*]? Well, the inhabited land is about to be invaded. The land dwelt on is going to be dwelt in. The tables are being turned. While Israel appears to be occupied by Rome, in reality her Messiah has come. He who is the real occupier of time, space, and men's hearts is revealed. That's why it was predicted and came to pass that this baby be called Emmanuel.

Emmanuel means “God with us.” When it looks like all is occupied by the enemy—God shows what real occupation is all about! This fun twist was predicted by Isaiah who said that the land dwelling in darkness will see a great light. He prophesied:

> The people who walked in darkness
> have seen a great light;
> those who lived in a land of deep darkness—
> on them light has shined. (Isaiah 9:2 NRSV)

John shares that Jesus is the light of the world, dwelling among us. Beginning his revelation about Jesus, John declares:

> The true light, which gives light to everyone, was coming into the world. (John 1:9 ESV)

That which was dark will be light. That which was dwelt on will be dwelt in by God. Luke is having lots of fun here, because he knows who the real occupier is. Luke knows Jesus.

A FUNNY HOMETOWN

Luke uncorks another great joke in verse 4:

> And Joseph also went up from Galilee, from the city of Nazareth, to Judea, to the city of David, which is called Bethlehem, because he was of the house and family of David (Luke 2:4 NASB)

Whoa! Joseph and Mary come from Nazareth and will eventually go back there to live with the boy. That means the Lord Almighty is going to be raised in Nazareth, the backwater of all Galilee. What a riot! This is a funny hometown for the King of the Universe. John's gospel illustrates how humble and incongruous this is for Jesus. John reports:

> Philip found Nathanael and said to him, "We have found Him of whom Moses in the Law and also the Prophets wrote, Jesus of Nazareth, the son of Joseph." And Nathanael said to him, "Can any good thing come out of Nazareth?" Philip said to him, "Come and see." (John 1:45-46 NASB)

When Philip goes to tell Nathanael that Jesus is the promised Messiah, Nathanael asks, "Can anything good come out of Nazareth?" Nazareth was close to many Hellenized Gentile settlements and was a frontier town in the region of Zebulun. That combination made zealous Israelites rather mistrustful of the village of Nazareth. It's just not the kind of place you'd expect the Messiah to be from, making Luke 2:4 sidesplitting funny to a Hebrew.

FUNNY FAMILY

Verse 5 is even more oddly hilarious:

> to be registered with Mary, his betrothed, who was with child. (Luke 2:5 ESV)

This is a funny kind of family: an unmarried man and an engaged woman already with child. According to Scripture, such isn't proper. Think about Mary traveling with her fiancé in that status through first century Israel. It would be highly irregular to say the least. In fact, by all rights in that time and place, Mary should be either dead or married. And the more one looks into the situation, the more the ironies pile up: they have to spend money traveling so they can register in order to—wait for it—spend more money in taxes; Joseph is sticking with his legally betrothed even though she was illegally pregnant; and Mary is with child though still a virgin.

And you thought your family was weird! God orchestrated this instant and odd family situation as His means to save the world. Such is the Lord's way. He tells us that He uses the foolish things of the world to shame the wise. [See 1 Corinthians 1:27.] Then God calls us to be like Mary and Joseph—to become willing fools for Jesus.

FUNNY AUDIENCE

After Jesus was born, angels appeared to shepherds outside Bethlehem. This section is also supposed to make us laugh even as it moves us in awe:

> In the same region, shepherds were staying out in the fields and keeping watch at night over their flock. Then an angel of the Lord stood before them, and the glory of the Lord shone around them, and they were terrified. But the angel said to them, "Don't be afraid, for look, I proclaim to you good news of great joy that will be for all the people: Today a Savior, who is Messiah the Lord, was born for you in the city of David. This will be the sign for you: You will find a baby wrapped snugly in cloth and lying in a feeding trough."
>
> Suddenly there was a multitude of the heavenly host with the angel, praising God and saying:

> Glory to God in the highest heaven,
> and peace on earth to people He favors!
>
> When the angels had left them and returned to heaven, the shepherds said to one another, "Let's go straight to Bethlehem and see what has happened, which the Lord has made known to us." They hurried off and found both Mary and Joseph, and the baby who was lying in the feeding trough. After seeing them, they reported the message they were told about this child, and all who heard it were amazed at what the shepherds said to them. (Luke 2:8-18 HCSB)

This is an odd audience for a cosmic miracle. As much as we revere shepherds in our romantic, pastoral minds, the reality is that sheep smell … and shepherds smell worse. Is this really the audience you would have picked to witness the greatest change moment in history? As the 4Him Christmas song says, "I'm not one to second-guess what angels have to say … but this is such a strange way to save the world."[8]

These are comical witnesses to go spread the good news of Messiah's birth. According to later Jewish sources, shepherds were not ceremonially clean according to the Law. There were places shepherds couldn't go, and they couldn't even testify in court. Admittedly, these sources are slanted and come five centuries after Jesus' birth; but even in the first century we know that shepherds were not known as great news-carriers. They spent much of their time apart from people, after all. It would be like Farmer Brown coming running up here with breaking news from the Pentagon. That's funny!

And God crafts it purposefully. He uses the humor to heighten the message and spread its impact. The people to whom the shepherds talked were challenged! "Wondered" in verse 18 is Luke's *ethaumasan* [ἐθαύμασαν]. It means "marveled" or "were astonished" and carries the idea of a challenge—especially the challenge miracles pose to human assumptions. These people around Bethlehem marveled because of the challenge of a miraculous birth announced by angels, and also because

8 David Allen Clark, Mark R. Harris, and Donald A. Koch, *Strange Way to Save the World*. 4Him. New Spring, 1994. CD.

these simple shepherds spoke with such depth of knowing. Look at the phrase "they made known" in verse 17. That is a fascinating word choice, where Dr. Luke uses a term for knowing that employs the Greek word *ginosko* [γινώσκω].

Ginosko—which we'll discuss further in a later chapter—is the word for deeply knowing something way down in your heart. It's the word used for how God knows us ... for sex in marriage ... and for understanding that is deep. The people were astonished because these shepherds really knew the truth of the Messiah. They knew it down deep and they shared it. By the way, we don't know exactly how the various people responded to the amazing insights of profound knowledge from the shepherds. *Ethaumasan* can refer to either critical skeptical wondering or enthusiastic astonishment that leads to worship. The author is supposed to add one of a few key words to *ethaumasan* so that we know which response it is in a situation—skepticism or worship. Luke refuses to add the normal words, adding dramatic tension and implying that the response was mixed.

THIS IS GOD'S TIMING.

If we go back up to the very beginning of verse 1 we read that a decree was made. Here's another idea connected to God's humility, but this one has a twist. The text makes clear what we see regularly in history: the big king thinks he's in charge. He tells people where to go, and crying "Yes sir!" they all go. Augustus says "register" by royal decree, and by golly, everybody registers.

That's what it looks like on the surface. But actually, Caesar Augustus is merely a tool being used by God. Augustus is really just a pawn, not the king. Augustus was the tool used by the true Master to get the real king to the place God had promised he would be born. [See Micah 5:2.] Chuck Swindoll does a great job emphasizing the import of this decree and how it actually reflects God's timing:

> The Roman Empire was as vast as it was vicious. Political intrigue, racial tension, increased immorality, and enormous military might occupied everyone's attention and conversation. Palestine existed under the crush of Rome's heavy boot. All eyes were on Augustus, the cynical Caesar who demanded

> a census so as to determine a measurement to enlarge taxes. At that time who was interested in a couple making an eighty-mile trip south from Nazareth? What could possibly be more important than Caesar's decisions in Rome? Who cared about a Jewish boy born in Bethlehem?
>
> God did. Without realizing it, mighty Augustus was only an errand boy for the fulfillment of Micah's prediction … a pawn in the hand of Yahweh … a piece of lint on the pages of prophecy. While Rome was busy making history, God arrived. He pitched His fleshly tent in silence on straw … in a stable … under a star. The world didn't even notice. Reeling in the wake of Alexander the Great … Herod the Great … Augustus the Great...the world overlooked Mary's little Lamb.
>
> It still does.[9]

Chuck understands Luke's funny contrast between Augustus and the real king, Jesus. God liked that hilarious contrast. Luke likes it too, because it shows who's really in charge. This is all about God's timing. The same emphasis is found in verse 6:

> While they were there, the days were completed for her to give birth. (Luke 2:6 NASB)

"The days were completed." This takes us once again to Luke's focus on time. He sees time as something controlled by God and passively experienced by humans. The Greek experts tell me that this construction is a really neat and rare use of terms. "Were completed" is from a common verb *eplesthesan* [ἐπλήσθησαν], but Luke uses it in a completely unique way in order to demonstrate that even time is passive.

Luke's point is that this is all utterly planned by God. In fact, every verb in the verse is passive in the Greek. In English it doesn't make sense to say literally what the Greek says. But it is important to notice that everything is passive here. The Greek actually reads, "were accomplished

9 Charles R. Swindoll, *Christ in Christmas: A Family Advent Celebration* (Colorado Springs: Navpress, 1989), 42.

days that should be delivered she." See? All the verbs are passive. God is in control and He wanted the birth to happen at that moment in that place for very important reasons.

The Triune God wanted even the birth of the Messiah to represent sacrifice. Even in His birth, Jesus was sacrificing to make room for people. Certainly God the Father could have arranged for the true report to have read: "And they were royally treated while others slept in the street." Yet God chose to arrive in flesh out in the stable, allowing others to enter the inn. Think about all the sacrifices in just this one short passage:

- The sacrifice of being human … phenomenal cosmic power, itty-bitty living space.
- The sacrifice of deprivations that night in the caravansary. She laid him in a manger.
- The sacrifice He had in mind all along. This is the Messiah, Christ, the Rescuer.

Jesus was born for a very specific purpose: to save your eternal soul. Remember how Isaiah pointed out that people walk in darkness and John described Jesus as light of the world? Well look at what Jesus Himself says in John 12:

> "I have come as light into the world, that everyone who believes in Me may not remain in darkness." (John 12:46 NASB)

Friend, if you have never trusted Jesus, please do so right now. Jesus sacrificed Himself on the cross and rose from the grave so that all of us who believe in Him are transferred into God's light. Jesus is undeniably true and everyone must wrestle with the reality that He came in Bethlehem. I pray you investigate thoroughly and reach the only reasonable conclusion—the wonder [*ethaumasan*] of worship.

OUR RESPONSE

The truth that Jesus came to sacrifice for people takes us to two appropriate responses from those who are Christians.

1. Find Christmas in *humility.* The humor, timing, and sacrifice work together to deepen the big idea that Jesus chooses humility as His means to implement Christmas. We can't help but be struck that humility is a major part of God's message. Is that the story of our Christmas?

   Please don't misunderstand. It is fine to feast and party. After all, the Bible commands and teaches us to celebrate! Even Jesus in his humility had a whole army of angels and a special star. The point isn't the size of your celebration but the *focus* of it. Humility has nothing to do with poverty, per se. The point of humility is focus. The humble person is thinking of the real meaning of the celebration and doesn't slip into the typical human trap of thinking it's all about self. The humble person is concerned with what she can give and how that blesses the Lord. As Dr. Luke's dear friend Paul wrote:

   > Do nothing from selfishness or empty conceit, but with humility of mind let each of you regard one another as more important than himself; do not merely look out for your own personal interests, but also for the interests of others. Have this attitude in yourselves which was also in Christ Jesus. (Philippians 2:3-5 NASB)

   Think of others as more than only yourself. This is part of what even our culture does at Christmas. Impressed by the humility of Christmas, non-Christians give gifts; they contribute to charity; they sacrifice. Surely if all these people trapped in darkness can imitate Jesus in sacrifice, then those who trust Him can become like Him and find Christmas in humility.

2. Share Christmas through *witness.* What did the shepherds do? They shared what was in their hearts. Those shepherds weren't trained. They just told the truth. The same

should be our *modus operandi.* Training is great, but not critical. All that's necessary is that we know Jesus and share with others what we know. One can give gospel tracts with Christmas presents, bring friends to the church's Christmas outreach, or take extended family to Christmas Eve services. Whatever you do, act on the truth deep in your heart. Share Christmas through your witness just as the shepherds did. (We'll discuss this a bit more later.)

O Little Town of Bethlehem
(Phillips Brooks[10])

O little town of Bethlehem
How still we see thee lie
Above thy deep and dreamless sleep
The silent stars go by
Yet in thy dark streets shineth
The everlasting Light
The hopes and fears of all the years
Are met in thee tonight

For Christ is born of Mary
And gathered all above
While mortals sleep, the angels keep
Their watch of wondering love
O morning stars together
Proclaim the holy birth
And praises sing to God the King
And Peace to men on earth

How silently, how silently
The wondrous gift is given!
So God imparts to human hearts
The blessings of His heaven.
No ear may hear His coming,
But in this world of sin,

10 Phillips Brooks, 1868. Public domain.

Where meek souls will receive him still,
The dear Christ enters in.

O holy Child of Bethlehem
Descend to us, we pray
Cast out our sin and enter in
Be born to us today
We hear the Christmas angels
The great glad tidings tell
O come to us, abide with us
Our Lord Emmanuel

THE SAVIOR OF CHRISTMAS

CHAPTER SUMMARY: The great New Testament scholar F. F. Bruce points out that *soter* [σωτὴρ] is a favorite word of Luke and Paul. It appears seldom outside their writings. However, to Luke, the word had significant nuances:

1. Savior. In the Septuagint Psalms, *soter* is used of the one who both physically and spiritually saves.
2. God-King. Roman citizens used the term of their Deified Emperors, adding an idea of god-ruler.

Luke is also completely exclusive in recording the angels' depiction of this newborn as *Christos Kurios* [χριστὸς κύριος]. While we can't be absolutely sure of the meaning because it appears nowhere else in literature, the word choices and combination indicate:

1. Lordship. Jesus is Lord, something Luke emphasizes throughout His accounts.
2. Anointing. Jesus is the Lord's anointed.

LIFE CHANGE OBJECTIVE: That we worship the Savior Lord of Christmas.

SO-AND-SO SAVES CHRISTMAS

Here's the easiest prediction ever made. Ready? During November and December this year, you will run into some book, TV special, movie, or other media story about how someone or something saves Christmas. It's a certainty, isn't it? A very quick search revealed to me stories about Elmo, Tractor Mac, Felix the Cat, Noddy, Rover, Diego, and Ernest each saving Christmas! When you see these special books, cartoons, and movies this winter, what do you think?

I think I'm going to throw up.

Please, don't go outside and burn your Christmas video collection. That's not the point. But do think it through. Look at the sentence above in bold: "So-and-so saves Christmas." An endless litany of names could be filled in. Every year there are new candidates, new stories that vie for our Christmas attention. Why is that? The Bible tells us that the world, our own selfishness, and our enemy Satan all want to direct worship away from Jesus. If we let all these things distract us from the real Savior of Christmas then the real Grinch, Satan, has his triumph.

So, whatever else you are bombarded with, be sure to understand this truth: there is one Savior of Christmas and His name is Jesus. If you want to watch how "the white squirrel of Christmas saved the holiday with the help of his woodland friends" that's cool—as long as you actively focus on the truth that there is only one savior of Christmas. He's not a squirrel, a snowman, a puppet, or even John McClane of the Die Hard films.

The Savior of Christmas is the God-man, Jesus. And the only way to save Christmas—or anything else—is to engage with Him.

THE REAL SAVIOR OF CHRISTMAS

> For today in the city of David there has been born for you a Savior, who is Christ the Lord. (Luke 2:11 NASB)

Luke uses some very curious terms, words that teach us a great deal about the real message of Christmas. And there are enough of Luke's special terms in this one verse to keep us busy learning for quite some time. Start with the second word there: today. This is the Greek *semeron* [σήμερον], a favorite word of Luke's. Bible textual scholar Daniel Wallace notes that Luke uses this term more than any other writer.[11]

Semeron occurs 11 times in Luke's gospel and 9 times in his book that we call *Acts*. In Luke's uses, *semeron* has a fascinating meaning. More than just one day, *semeron* signifies the dawning of an age. This was not a meaning Luke designed. It was employed by other authors as well. However, Luke *only* uses *semeron* of an epoch or age—specifically the age of Messiah. So when the angel says, "Today," it's addressing more than just a day. This is *the* Day. Luke isn't just recording a word that came from an angel during one 24-hour period. He is highlighting the beginning of an entirely new era.

I was blessed to grow up with a wonderful pastor who taught us this. I understood what Luke is telling us: that Jesus' birth is the dawn of an entirely new age. So, imagine my joy when I went to college and met a bunch of nice kids going to what they called "New Age" meetings. I thought, "Cool!" I was really impressed with the name "New Age," assuming that indicated people who understood the huge change meant by Luke's word "today." I went to that first meeting expecting to hear all about our new lives in Jesus, the Savior of Christmas. I left early, very disappointed. You no doubt would have known what I quickly discovered—that those New Agers had no interest in the Bible or Jesus.

FULFILLMENT OF PROPHECY

In fact, the so-called "New Agers" miss completely the reality of the New Age. Scripture reveals two big aspects of this new Messianic age. First is the fulfillment of prophecy. This is a very big deal to Luke, who cares that the record is clear and precise. For example, consider how Luke begins his gospel:

> Inasmuch as many have undertaken to compile a narrative of the things that have been accomplished among us, just as those who from the beginning were eyewitnesses and ministers of the word have delivered them to us, it seemed good to me

11 Daniel Wallace, "Luke: Introduction, Outline, and Argument." *Bible.org*. N.p., n.d. Web. 17 Nov. 2008.

> also, having followed all things closely for some time past, to write an orderly account for you, most excellent Theophilus, that you may have certainty concerning the things you have been taught. (Luke 1:1-4 ESV)

Luke is a careful student of the intricate fulfillment of prophecy that has led to "today" [*semeron*]. We see this focus on fulfilled prophecy continued throughout the book. Later in Luke chapter 1, Mary is told that she will miraculously fulfill Isaiah's prophecy and that she will give birth even though she's a virgin. Luke records how Mary then goes to see her relative Elizabeth, who is also with child. Look at Elizabeth's great statement about Mary and the Messiah she carries:

> In those days Mary arose and went with haste into the hill country, to a town in Judah, and she entered the house of Zechariah and greeted Elizabeth. And when Elizabeth heard the greeting of Mary, the baby leaped in her womb. And Elizabeth was filled with the Holy Spirit, and she exclaimed with a loud cry, "Blessed are you among women, and blessed is the fruit of your womb! And why is this granted to me that the mother of my Lord should come to me? For behold, when the sound of your greeting came to my ears, the baby in my womb leaped for joy. And blessed is she who believed that there would be a fulfillment of what was spoken to her from the Lord." (Luke 1:39-45 ESV)

Focus on the last sentence and the word "fulfillment." This verbiage pulls out the truth for us, emphasizing that this Messianic Age is all about the fulfillment of prophecy. In fact, Mary's beautiful speech in reply to Elizabeth is riddled with fulfilled prophecy. She quotes extensively from the Old Testament, highlighting her understanding that this is a new age. "Today" is a new age—an age where prophecy is fulfilled!

SALVATION BY GOD'S GRACE THROUGH THE MESSIAH

The second aspect of this New Age involves salvation by God's grace through the Messiah. Of course, salvation has *always* been by God's grace through faith. We see this displayed from the beginning with Abraham. In

Genesis, God proclaims that "Abram believed the Lord, and He credited it to him as righteousness." (Genesis 15:6 HCSB) But God promised that one day grace would be expressed through a Messiah who would come to the world through Abraham's line.

Consider again God's word to Father Abraham alongside Mary's great cry recorded by Luke:

> "Abram believed the LORD, and He credited it to him as righteousness." (Genesis 15:6 HCSB)
>
> "He has given help to Israel His servant,
> In remembrance of His mercy,
> As He spoke to our fathers,
>
> To Abraham and his descendants forever." (Luke 1:54-55 NASB)

Mary perceives and Luke highlights that salvation by God's grace through faith now has a specific face—a Savior sent to begin the new age of the Messiah. Luke's ministry partner, Paul, became the Holy Spirit's great spokesman for this. As Luke and Paul traveled and wrote and taught together, Paul would speak and write out the truth in letter after letter. Luke would also record the truth in passages like this:

> There is salvation in no one else, for there is no other name under heaven given among mortals by which we must be saved." (Acts 4:12 NRSV)

Salvation is by God's grace through faith in the Messiah Jesus—that is what "today" means.

On August 1, 1774, Joseph Priestly burned mercuric oxide in a glass tube. The gas created was different, and Priestly called it "dephlogisticated air." He wrote, "It might be peculiarly salutary for the lungs." He was right. Thankfully, the French chemist Antoine Lavoisier gave Priestly's dephlogisticated air another name—he called it oxygen. Though Priestly was a poor name-giver, he was right on about the positive effects of oxygen. Oxygen is salutary, even critical, for life. Later, Priestly also discovered nitrogen, nitrous oxide (I'll bet he laughed over that one—sorry, I couldn't resist), hydrogen chloride, and ammonia.

Oxygen was always there before Priestly, but he opened up a whole new age. After his discovery there was a specific understanding about what it was that made life possible on earth. In a similar way, Jesus was the Savior all along, but thanks to Luke we now know His name. Now we understand Who makes life possible on earth and in heaven—the prophecy-fulfilling Messiah that opens up a new age "today."

SAVIOR

Luke writes : For today in the city of David there has been born for you a Savior, who is Christ the Lord. (Luke 2:11 NASB) These are power-packed words in Luke 2:11. Think about the noun Savior. The Great Scottish scholar F. F. Bruce points out that the Greek word for Savior—*soter* [σωτὴρ]—is a favorite word of Luke & Paul. In fact, not only do Luke and Paul use *soter* a lot, but the term appears seldom in scripture outside of their writings.[12] I think Luke, brilliant writer that he was, loved *soter* because the word has significant nuances beyond just "savior."

RESCUER

First, as a careful student of Hebrew culture, Luke knows that *soter* means "rescuer." Amazingly, Luke the Gentile understood and even used Hebrew. It seems likely that Luke primarily read the Old Testament in the Greek translation called the Septuagint. That's important because in the Septuagint Psalms (the Greek translation of the Psalms), *soter* is the rare term used of one who both physically and spiritually saves. The Septuagint uses *soter* for a rescuer. In fact, David uses *soter* to refer to God the Rescuer.

So, when Luke records the angel in verse 11 crying out that this baby is *soter*, we learn that Jesus is the Rescuer! Further, thinking back to the way *soter* is used by David, we deduce that Jesus is the *Divine* Rescuer.

On December 5, 1986, Walter Wyatt tried to fly from Nassau to Miami. It was an unfortunate trip, as a storm and equipment failure forced Walter to cry mayday. A Coast Guard Falcon search plane came to guide him to a landing strip, but Walter's engine failed while he was still six miles out over the sea. He crashed into the Caribbean just as night fell.

12 F. F. Bruce, *The Canon of Scripture* (Downer's Grove, IL: InterVarsity Press, 1988), 178.

Amazingly, Walter survived, floating in a leaky life vest watching the cuts on his body turn the water around him red. As you might expect, sharks gathered. For ten hours, Walter kicked the sharks away. Finally, the Coast Guard Cutter *Cape York* found Walter Wyatt. The cutter scared away the sharks and hauled Walter up to safety. Now, how do you think Walter responded? The same way anyone would: he fell on the deck and kissed it. He shook the hand of every Coastie. He thanked the rescuers.

Is that our response to Jesus this Christmas? He is the Divine Rescuer! We who were slated for shark-bait are amazingly rescued by God's grace through faith in the epoch-altering Messiah. Yet, we seem to spend precious little time praising our Rescuer. In the midst of our busy holiday, we are prone to forget just what *soter* means.

GOD-KING

There's a second aspect of what Savior means in Luke 2:11. *Soter* also means God-King. You see, Greek-speaking Roman citizens used the term *soter* of their deified emperors. Whenever the Roman Senate felt so inclined, they would declare a former (or more rarely, a current) emperor to be a god. Often a temple would be erected. For example, my family once had a picnic lunch in the ruins of the "Temple to the Divine Julius Caesar" on Rome's ancient Via Sacra. In Greek, they called that building *soter hieron* [σωτὴρ ἱερὸν], which meant "God-King's Temple."

Understanding that, we realize that in Luke 2 God is being pretty sarcastic! And He of course uses Luke, the writer with a rapier wit and grand sense of humor, to record it. Luke says, "You think you are so important. Your *soter*, your god-kings are dead, declared only by men, and revered in cold marble. That's so pitiful. Here's how it's really done!" Luke points to Jesus and proves that *this* is the real God-King. Not Julius … not Herod … not Augustus … this warm, living, little baby born in a dirt stable is declared God-King by angels. That declaration trumps any old Senate. Jesus is the *Soter*! This makes Jesus the most important thing of all. He is the true reason for the season, the Rescuer and God-King.

Sadly, most of the world missed that. They were too busy declaring their own god-kings. Thank goodness we're not like that! Or are we?

I have a horrible tendency to forget that Jesus is the Rescuer and God-King, and I doubt I am alone among believers in Christ. Sometimes,

I worry over politics, fretting about American elections and what happens in European Union elections. Other days I make my children the god-kings and act as if what they get for Christmas is the most important thing in the universe.

God laughs at all that. Through Luke's pen, He laughs at me and all the rest of the knuckleheads on this planet and says, "Look. Here's the *Soter*." Jesus is the Rescuer and the God-King. All the other stuff of life—good, bad, and indifferent—must not be allowed to distract from the real king of Christmas. As J. I. Packer points out:

> As the second person of the Trinity, co-creator with the Father, Christ is the eternal king over all things. As Savior, He is the king of a spiritual kingdom—that is, He rules in the hearts and lives of His people … Christ rules and governs all things on behalf of His church. He will not allow His purposes to be frustrated in the end … He will deliver this kingdom to the Father when He accomplishes the final victory over evil (1 Cor. 15:24-28), i.e., when He destroys this world order once and for all and makes it new … No human kings or diabolical powers will be able to reign. Only Christ and His Kingdom will be preserved.[13]

Jesus is Rescuer and God-King. Amen! Now, ruminate again on verse 11, this time in the English Standard Version translation:

> For unto you is born this day in the city of David a Savior, who is Christ the Lord. (Luke 2:11 ESV)

CHRISTOS

Luke is completely exclusive in recording the angels' depiction of this newborn as Christ the Lord. This is a singular construction: *Christos Kurios* [χριστὸς κύριος]. The words have an interesting history upon which Luke is drawing. The Greek word *Christos* = Messiah from Hebrew and is drawing on the long lineage of that term in Hebrew.

13 J. I. Packer, *Celebrating the Saving Work of God: Collected Shorter Writings of J. I. Packer on the Trinity, Christ, and the Holy Spirit* (Milton Keynes, UK: Paternoster Publishing, 1998), 41.

Early in Jewish history, the word messiah just meant "anointed." It's a term that meant knowledge, especially having an inside track of knowledge. Thus, when someone was anointed with oil it always involved a prophecy or declaration of information; e.g., David was proclaimed future king of Israel when anointed by Samuel. A little later in the Old Testament era, the expression messiah began to depict "an anointed *one.*" Here the concept became some person set aside to do special tasks with their knowledge. This meaning has a parallel in U.S. history. There is a private journal in which every U.S. President has written. Only U.S. Presidents are allowed to read the book, and that special inside knowledge is separate from all the rest of us. The President is special. Out of 300,000,000 Americans, only he is "an anointed one" in this sense.

Later, some years after David's death and the breakup of Israel into two kingdoms, messiah was used for "*the* anointed one." This slight change in usage meant messiah is not just anybody who gets elected for special knowledge and work. It's a very special, singular person who is the anointed. This singularity becomes key to uses of "messiah" in the later Old Testament prophets.

During the inter-testament period of 400 years between the conclusion of the Old Testament and the writing of the New Testament, when Greek became the world's language, the idea of anointed morphed again. To the Hebrews of those centuries just before Jesus' birth, messiah became "the *hoped-for* anointed one." Here the term becomes very specific. There is only one right person, only one Messiah sent from God. He must fit clear prophetic parameters established by God's Word.[14]

As this idea grew in Jewish society, many people found it convenient to rise up and claim to be the Messiah, the Christ, the hoped-for anointed

14 A theologian friend of mine thinks Luke could be drawing from the close parallel phrase in Lamentation 4:20. There "Messiah YHWH" is used as a construction to describe Jeremiah's lamentation that Jerusalem will see even more destruction—the downfall of a Messiah in whom the Jews thought they would finally find freedom. If that is in mind, then Luke is making clever commentary here. Jesus is that Messiah Jeremiah foresaw. He is the Lord's anointed, Messiah YHWH, *Christos Kurios*. He will indeed fall into destruction as foretold. However, the angels show that Jesus is more than what Jeremiah could see. Jesus is the real *Soter*. He will pay the price for salvation and rise from the grave as Savior, Deified Emperor, Lord, and Anointed One.

one. That's why the first century B.C. experienced so many false Messiahs. None of them fit the very precise prophecies associated with the Christ, but the lure of fame kept many trying to pretend they were the Messiah. Inevitably, the people who followed them became quickly disillusioned, disappointed, or dead.

Luke is aware of all this and has it in mind when, in the mid-first century A.D., he uses the word *Christos*. Christ means the hoped-for anointed one. When the angel speaks this monumental description by calling the baby *Christos*, everyone in Palestine knows what that means. Luke records this power-packed word so that Gentiles can understand as well. God wants Gentiles to know that Jesus is the right train to board. He is indeed the one and only hoped-for anointed one.

KURIOS

The other part of Luke's unique construction *Christos Kurios* [χριστὸς κύριος] is *Kurios*. Thus, my little wordplay in calling this study "Luke's Curious Christmas." We actually wanted to title the book *Luke's Kurios Xristmas,* but feared that might break Google if people searched for it. *Kurios* of course doesn't mean curious. It's a great Greek term for "Lord."

Of course, Luke's word choice is also curious with a "c" because no other author had ever combined these two words into the phrase *Christos Kurios*. God is having Luke do something unique here. He's indicating that the hoped-for one born in Bethlehem is actually Lord of all. In fact, this is a drum Luke beats regularly as the Lordship of Jesus is emphasized throughout the gospel.

This is so important that Luke can't overstate it. Jesus is Lord. He is meant to be Lord of your life and my life. Christians are not supposed to live like and look like all the rest of the world. Such is ridiculous because we have a Lord who is over our lives; a *Kurios* who is singular and holy *Christos*. Following Him, we are to grow in His singularity and holiness.

In the film *Talladega Nights* there is a scene where the comedic NASCAR star Ricky Bobby leads in prayer. He keeps saying over and over "Baby Jesus … thank you Baby Jesus." He only calls the Lord "Baby Jesus." The scene is painful to watch (something many felt was true of the entire film). However, that prayer has a really important lesson. Even after his wife corrects him, the self-centered star only prays to "Baby Jesus." He confesses that he prefers the *Baby* Jesus. Why? Because he doesn't want to bow before the Jesus who is Lord. This clown thinks that keeping Jesus a baby in his mind allows him to avoid the fact of *Christos Kurios*. He can avoid the implications of talking to One who is truly Lord.

Friends, we are too much like that! Most Christians need a reminder that the baby Jesus comes as the genuine Lord. Jesus is the Messiah who opens a new era of salvation by grace. He is also the Lord, the God-King who knows all and who allows the rescued to know God.

SO, HOW DOES ALL THAT AFFECT US?

Two specific responses jumped to my mind as I read Luke 2:11. Please don't limit yourself to my applications, as the Holy Spirit will likely inspire even more responses for you. For me, I read this and I am moved to:

1. **Respond to His Lordship**. Jesus is Lord. I dare not let a Christmas go by without stopping and resetting my heart on this reality—Jesus is Lord. I must stop stumbling around, following everything but Jesus. I must respond to who He really is. After all, He pursues me, reaching down from heaven to engage me in His love. As Werner Foerster writes in his article on *Kurios* in *The Theological Dictionary of the New Testament:*

   > Man is confronted in God the Creator by One who … is the absolute authority before which it is freedom rather than bondage to bow. In [*Kurios*] … a humanity which has rejected subordination to its Creator is confronted by the One who with the authority of the ministering and forgiving love of God woos its obedience and reconstructs all the relations of lordship.[15]

2. **Live in light of our new era and eternity to come**. In Jesus, we are shown part of the mystery of time. We know this

15 G. Kittel, G., Bromiley, G. W., & Friedrich, G., eds. *Theological Dictionary of the New Testament* (electronic ed., Vol. 3, 1040). Grand Rapids, MI: Eerdmans,1964.

isn't the end. This is merely one era. Jesus is coming back to fulfill the rest of prophecy. He will establish His kingdom. Knowing that, I can live differently. Jude 24-25 summarizes how Jesus' Lordship causes me to live in light of eternity.

> Now unto him that is able to keep you from falling, and to present *you* faultless before the presence of his glory with exceeding joy, to the only wise God our Saviour, *be* glory and majesty, dominion and power, both now and ever. Amen. (Jude 24-25 KJV)

Finally, there is one other response that I fervently pray for anyone reading this who is not a believer in Jesus:

3. **Receive His rescue**. If you have never trusted Jesus as Savior, do so now. Salvation comes by God's grace through faith in Jesus. He willingly came and died on a cross so that you might be rescued by His death and resurrection. Jesus died as a perfect sacrifice, taking your place, paying for your sins even though He was sinless. Why did He do this? Because He loves you! He wanted to rescue you, knowing that we humans are defaced by sin and unable to rescue ourselves. Do you know what present Jesus wants for Christmas? You. He wants you to be saved by believing in Him. Right now, confess your trust in Jesus.

Hark the Herald Angels Sing
(Charles Wesley[16])

Hark! the herald angels sing,
"Glory to the new born King,
peace on earth, and mercy mild,
God and sinners reconciled!"
Joyful, all ye nations rise,
join the triumph of the skies;

16 Charles Wesley, with additions by George Whitefield. 1739. Public domain.

with th' angelic host proclaim,
"Christ is born in Bethlehem!"
Hark! the herald angels sing,
"Glory to the new born King!"

Christ, by highest heaven adored;
Christ, the everlasting Lord;
late in time behold him come,
offspring of a virgin's womb.
Veiled in flesh the Godhead see;
hail th' incarnate Deity,
pleased as man with man to dwell,
Jesus, our Emmanuel.
Hark! the herald angels sing,
"Glory to the new born King!"

Hail the heaven-born Prince of Peace!
Hail the Sun of Righteousness!
Light and life to all he brings,
risen with healing in his wings.
Mild he lays his glory by,
born that man no more may die,
born to raise the sons of earth,
born to give us second birth.
Hark! the herald angels sing,
"Glory to the new born King!"

Come, Desire of nations, come,
fix in us thy humble home;
rise, the woman's conquering Seed,
bruise in us the serpent's head.
Adam's likeness, Lord, efface;
stamp thine image in its place.
Second Adam from above,
Reinstate us in thy love.
Hark! the herald angels sing,
"Glory to the new born King!"

CHAPTER 4

THE WORD OF CHRISTMAS

CHAPTER SUMMARY: Luke teaches a great deal about knowledge in these verses. We'll focus on one special word, *rhema* [ῥῆμα] and its parallel term, *logos* [λόγος]. *Rhema* is a Hebraic-rooted idea that means "word" or "thing done." Through the shepherds, Luke declares that Jesus is the thing; He's the Word of Christmas. Our study of *rhema* will reveal these awesome attributes:

- The word judges.
- The word purifies.
- Belief comes through the word.
- The word is the agent of rebirth.

LIFE CHANGE OBJECTIVE: That we live according to the Word of Christmas.

THE IMPORTANCE OF SPECIFIC WORDING

As a professor, I have graded many tests and papers. Like all teachers, I have chuckled my way through many entertaining answers—both intentional and accidental. My personal favorite was the title of a dissertation I was grading. A witty veterinarian discussing specifics of using MRI technology for small animals named his study "There's More Than One Way to Scan a Cat."[17]

Some time ago, a friend who teaches mathematics sent me some hilarious test answers. Over the ensuing years, these have become staples of social media. I have no idea whether any are genuine, but they sure resemble a lot of my answers on math tests over the years.

The first one says "Expand" and then gives the problem (a+b)n. The student Peter just rewrote the problem wider and wider down the page. He expanded. The teacher wrote "Very funny, Peter." She then counted it wrong.

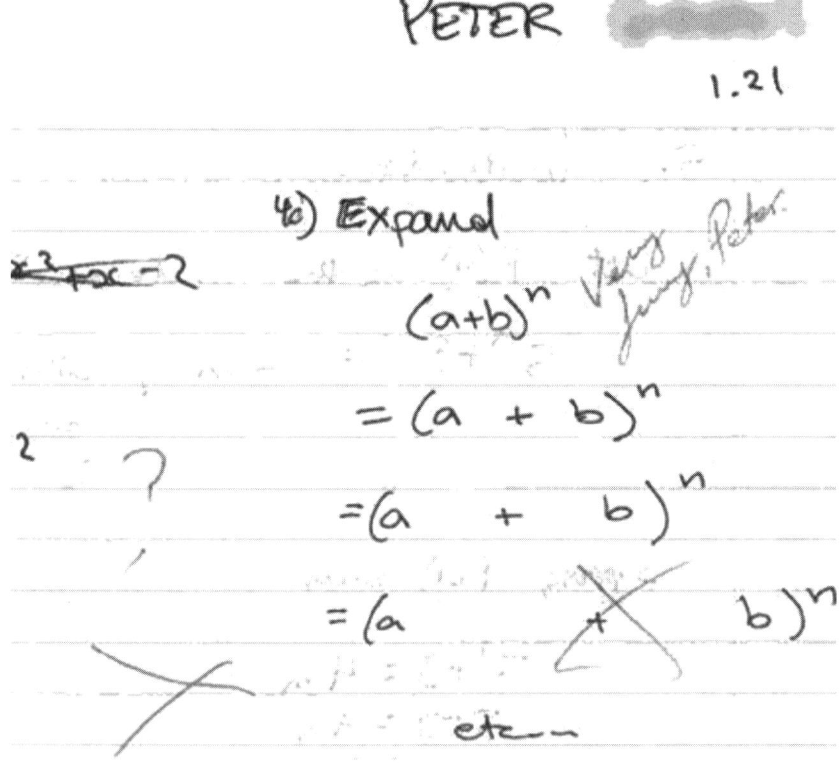

17 Christopher R. Lamb, "There's More Than One Way to Scan a Cat." London: Middlesex University, 2006.

The second question has a graphed curve for mass over time. The question reads, "Explain the shape of the graph." The student's reply struck me as genius:

> It's curvy, with a higher bit at the end and a rather aesthetically pleasing slope downwards toward a pretty flat strait (sic) bit. The actual graph itself consists of 2 strait lines meeting at the lower left hand corner of the graph and moving away at a 90-degree angle. Each line has an arrowhead on the end.

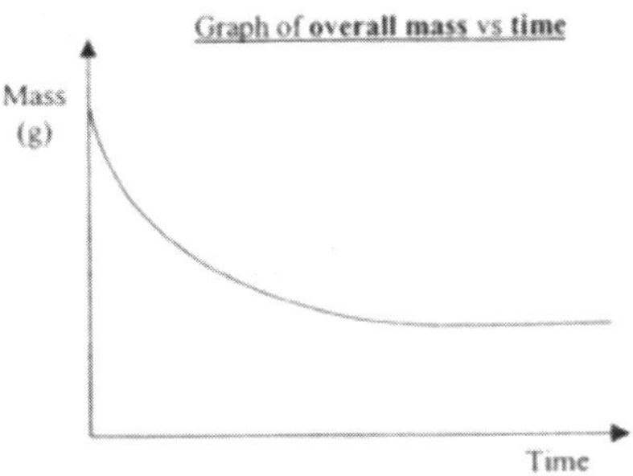

1. **Explain the shape of the graph.**

Its curvy, with a higher bit at the end and a rather aesthetically pleasing slope downwards towards a pretty flat strait bit. The actual graph itself consists of 2 strait lines meeting at the lower left hand corner of the graph and moving away at a 90° angle. Each line has an arrow head on the end.

One more—the best test answer I've ever seen. It involves a question for which the teacher says, "Find X." The student circles the x and says, "Here it is!"

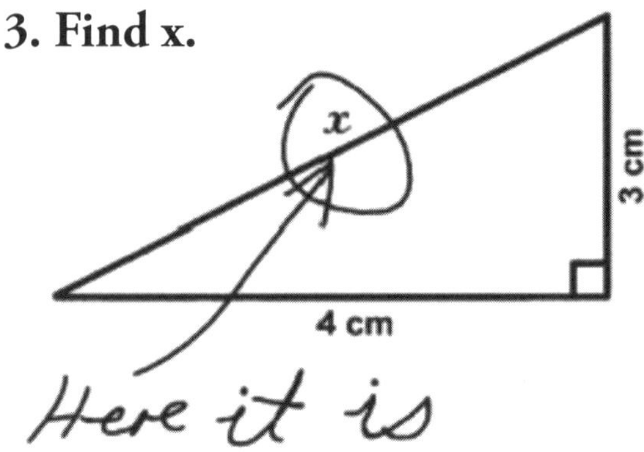

Notice the common theme in each situation. The teachers weren't specific enough in their words. I know, the students were ducking out, but the wording really wasn't explicit on those test questions. As one who used to teach school, I can testify to the importance of specific wording. You have to make sure things are very clear. Of course, they are math and science people, so possibly these teachers aren't the greatest at word power. (Sorry, I couldn't resist the opportunity to taunt!)

With that in mind, do you know what's really cool? God used a math and science guy—a physician—to record some the most intricate, explicit, and important words ever written. The doctor's name was Luke, and he really understood word power. In his writing, Luke made sure the specific meanings were clear.

We see this in much of Luke's narrative and especially in Luke 2:13-15:

> Suddenly there was a multitude of the heavenly host with the angel, praising God and saying:
>
> Glory to God in the highest heaven,
> and peace on earth to people He favors!

> When the angels had left them and returned to heaven, the shepherds said to one another, "Let's go straight to Bethlehem and see what has happened, which the Lord has made known to us." (Luke 2:13-15 HCSB)

RHEMA

In these verses, Luke teaches a great deal about word power. We're going to get to the heart of that teaching by dealing with one very significant word. In verse 15, Luke chooses a very curious term. *Rhema* [ῥῆμα] is what we translate "thing." There were other words for "thing." For example, he could have used the Greek *pragma*, from which we get the English pragmatic. That would have made sense. "Let us go see this matter, this *pragma*." But God has Luke record the shepherds specifically using the term *rhema*. Why?

Because Luke is teaching us; reaching us deeply. Even though *rhema* was used for "thing" in first-century conversation, the term *rhema* isn't as simple as just "thing." *Rhema* is a very weird word. It's actually a Hebraic slang of a Greek word. And like most slang, it has a morphed meaning; that is, it originally meant one thing but came to signify more. To understand, think of the English word "cool." Officially, what does cool mean? Right—chilly. But in accepted use, it also carries the idea of "popular" or "fun."

The earliest uses of *rhema* indicated a meaning of "word" or "saying" with this caveat—the word itself is the completion. *Rhema* is the word that makes things get done. *Rhema* was the term Hebrew people used for a Greek army officer's commands. When he said the word, it was done. This "something said, something done" concept explains how *rhema* became slang for "thing." When the word is spoken, the power is released and the thing is done.

You are probably familiar with the classic story *Mary Poppins* by E. L. Travers. Janna and I saw the stage version when I was teaching in London a few years ago, and it was super. Speaking of super, one of the great scenes in the stage and movie versions involves the Sherman brothers' musical depiction of "Supercalifragilisticexpialidocious." In the story this is a word of power. You say it and things are immediately changed. Remove the silly magic nonsense, and Supercalifragilisticexpialidocious is *rhema*. The word is spoken and things are changed.

Luke is being incredibly purposeful in his account. Earlier in verse 15, he relates that the shepherds "said." That is the Greek *elaloun* [ἐλάλουν], an obscure and nearly obsolete way to express speaking. It would be like me writing today, "I *voiced* to my companions … " And back in verse 13 the angels are "saying" something. "Saying" there is the Greek verb *legonton* [λεγόντων]. In *Koine* Greek, *legonton* indicated someone speaking a considered or practiced speech. [Note, my wife says *legonton* could also easily refer to the weight of all the Lego building toys in our play closet.]

Luke is going out of his way to make *rhema* singular; to set it apart amongst all these other words for words. The others are stilted, fancy words. The angels give a declaration. Even shepherds say an obsolete word, "I voice to thee … " Then, suddenly Luke unleashes this slang word *rhema*. "Let's see this thing … this Word from God … this *rhema*." His point appears to be that the word of Christmas is more than mere syllables. It is activity from a God who creates by the word of His mouth.

God's Word is the thing. Jesus is born. He is the Word. And that is the thing. At Christmas it is so easy to lose sight of the real thing, the *rhema*. We get caught up in parties and shopping and events and family. Are all those fine? Sure. They are even important. Are any of those the thing? No. Luke shows us all that matters is "this *rhema* the Lord has made known to us." Salvation has come in Jesus. Something said, something done. Jesus is God's Word and God's Word is the thing.

LOGOS

Rhema is somewhat similar to the more well-known Greek word *logos* [λόγος]. They are alike in that each means word and reason. John uses *logos* often, as in the beautiful opening of his gospel:

> In the beginning was the Word (*Logos*), and the Word was with God, and the Word was God … All things came into being through Him, and apart from Him nothing came into being that has come into being … And the Word became flesh, and dwelt among us, and we saw His glory, glory as of the only begotten from the Father, full of grace and truth … No one has seen God at any time; the only begotten God who

> is in the bosom of the Father, He has explained *Him.* (John 1:1,3,14,18 NASB)

John loves the *logos* idea and pictures it brilliantly. Luke prefers *rhema.* They are similar in that each term is willful, reasonable, and mindful. Why is this important? Because by describing the coming of Jesus as *rhema* and *logos* the gospel writers are telling us that Jesus is word and reason. John calls Jesus the Word. Luke calls Jesus' the thing. Each is saying that Jesus is the reasonable Word of God come to earth.

Scholar Dr. William Barclay wandered from biblical truth in some areas of his teaching. Nonetheless, he was a genius when it came to examining the Greek texts. He wrote:

> Jesus is the creating power of God come to men. He does not only *speak* the word of *knowledge*; he *is* the word of *power*. He did not come so much to *say* things to us as to *do* things for us. Jesus is also the incarnate mind (reason) of God. We might well translate John's words, 'The mind of God became a man.' A word is always 'the expression of a thought' and Jesus is the perfect expression of God's thought for men.[18]

THE WORD IS TRUE.

With that in mind, we see how deep a calling Luke was issuing by using *rhema.* He was tying into certain realities inherent in the idea of God's Word. One of these realities attested throughout scripture is that the word is true. Luke drives this home in Acts 26:

> And as he [the Apostle Paul] was saying these things in his defense, Festus said with a loud voice, "Paul, you are out of your mind; your great learning is driving you out of your mind." But Paul said, "I am not out of my mind, most excellent Festus, but I am speaking true and rational words. For the king knows about these things, and to him I speak boldly. For I am persuaded that none of these things has escaped his notice, for this has not been done in a corner. King Agrippa,

18 William Barclay, *New Testament Words* (Louisville, KY: Westminster, 1962), 182.

> do you believe the prophets? I know that you believe." And Agrippa said to Paul, "In a short time would you persuade me to be a Christian?" And Paul said, "Whether short or long, I would to God that not only you but also all who hear me this day might become such as I am—except for these chains." (Acts 26:24-29 ESV)

This hearing occurs when Paul is on trial for supposed sedition against Rome. Paul stands before Festus, the Roman governor at Caesarea, and Herod Agrippa, who bears the title "king" of the Roman province of Judea. Paul has been falsely accused, and even though the Jewish religious leaders hired a fancy Roman attorney, Luke records how Paul the scholar proves his innocence here. But Luke, as usual, is doing more than reporting the facts. Luke brings out how Paul isn't just defending himself, but actually making a convincing case for the gospel of Jesus.

It's a case so convincing that Herod Agrippa finds it necessary to dance around what is obviously true. Paul's word is true. Herod knows it and he has to resort to a kind of joke to keep from dealing with God's truth. The New Living Translation does a nice job with Herod Agrippa's poor attempt at humor:

> Agrippa interrupted him. "Do you think you can persuade me to become a Christian so quickly?" (Acts 26:28 NLT)

Why does Herod feel the need to sidestep Paul's question like that? Because the gospel Paul shares is true, and truth makes these bigwigs very uncomfortable. Luke's recording of Paul's speech in verse 25 makes that clear: "I am speaking true and rational words." "Words" is a form of Luke's expression *rhema*. The good news of Jesus Christ is the sober truth. It is based on things—*rhema*—that are fact. The Word is true.

THE WORD JUDGES.

Another reason humans try to duck God's truth is that once we recognize something is true we have no choice but to accept our accountability. In other words, the word judges. Ponder the penetrating statement of this in Hebrews 4:

> For the word of God is living and active and sharper than any two-edged sword, and piercing as far as the division of soul and spirit, of both joints and marrow, and able to judge the thoughts and intentions of the heart. (Hebrews 4:12 NASB)

The Word of God judges. It pierces our nonsensical rationalizations and surgically cuts us with needed truth. God's Word judges and His people respond to it. It never fails. One of the best parts of pastoring is seeing this dynamic in many different lives. The new Christian writes to me and says, "I just realized that I should be giving. I'm reading the Bible and it talks about giving an offering. How do I do that?" The young adult comes up after church and says, "Oh my goodness, pastor. I shouldn't be sleeping with my girlfriend! I see that is wrong according to what God says!" The mature Christian tells her Life Group, "I need to apologize. I was reading the Bible yesterday and a statement about gossip hit me right between the eyes."

The word judges. Luke is tapping in to that condition in order to describe Jesus. Jesus is the Word, and the word judges.

THE HEIGHT OF THE WORD IS BEYOND EXPRESSION.

Second Corinthians 12 explains another amazing aspect of the word of God:

> I know a man in Christ who fourteen years ago was caught up to the third heaven—whether in the body or out of the body I do not know, God knows. And I know that this man was caught up into paradise—whether in the body or out of the body I do not know, God knows—and he heard things that cannot be told, which man may not utter. (2 Corinthians 12:2 4 ESV)

The height of the word is beyond expression. In the context, Paul is talking about boasting and he uses this illustration of someone who was given a particular vision of heaven. The big idea in 2 Corinthians is that even this awesome vision isn't worthy of boasting. For our purposes, look at the verbiage Paul used. "Things that cannot be told" employs a form of *rhema*.

Caught up in heaven, there were words … things … *rhema* that cannot be expressed. This is an important and fascinating truth. God uses words to express Himself to us, but the real heart of the matter cannot be fully understood here on earth. Things that have to do with God's Word, with Jesus, cannot be completely captured by human words. It is indescribable. Chris Tomlin relates the idea in his worship song:

> Indescribable, uncontainable,
> You placed the stars in the sky and You know them by name.
> You are amazing God.
> All powerful, untamable,
> Awestruck we fall to our knees as we humbly proclaim,
> "You are amazing God."[19]

The height of God's Word—His *rhema*—is beyond expression. It's indescribable.

I was discussing this with a member of our church pulpit team and he said, "It's somewhat like talking to your pet." I was intrigued, and he expanded: "We can express truly deep emotions, and the pet 'understands' in some way, but the pet cannot really grasp the nuances of ideas. I say to my dog, 'Fluffy, I'm really moved by the *rhema* we discussed at church today.' His ears go up and Fluffy says, 'Woof?' but that's about it. He can tell something exciting went on, but he can't really reason through Luke with you." So is the ultimate height of God's Word to us.

THE WORD IS THE AGENT OF REBIRTH.

What we noted above is not to suggest that God's words are incomprehensible or that He doesn't reveal Himself to us. He does, and His Word is the agent of our rebirth to everlasting life. Such is the point in John 6:68.

> Simon Peter answered Him, "Lord, to whom shall we go? You have words of eternal life. (John 6:68 NASB)

19 Laura Story, Laura. *Indescribable*. Chris Tomlin. Six Steps, 2004. CD.

Jesus has the words of life. It is the words of Jesus that bring salvation. As you can likely guess, the term John recorded Peter using is a form of the Jewish-Greek slang *rhema.*

Not too long before Luke and John wrote, a scholar named Philo was also scrutinizing Hebrew and Greek wordplay. From his study in Alexandria, Egypt, Philo noted how often Hebrew and Greek influenced each other. Philo was especially struck by the idea of the "Word of God," writing, "The Word is the High Priest which sets the soul before God" and "The Word is the bridge between man and God."[20]

Philo was getting to something that Peter, Luke, and John would make clear: Jesus is the Word and the Word is life. Salvation comes through the *rhema* of Jesus ... the logos of God.

Sergeant Jacob DeShazer was an American pilot who joined Colonel Doolittle's famous and daring raids on Japan in April 1942. After the war, he related this remarkable story to his friend Don Falkenberg:

> When I flew as a member of ... Doolittle's squadron on the first raid over Japan my heart was filled with bitter hatred for the people of that nation. When our plane ran out of gas, and the members of the crew of my plane had to parachute down into Japanese-held territory in China and were captured by the enemy, the bitterness of my heart against my captors seemed more than I could bear.
>
> Taken to Tokyo with the survivors of another of our planes, we were imprisoned and beaten, half-starved, and denied by solitary confinement even the comfort of association with one another. Three of my buddies were executed by a firing squad about six months after our capture, and fourteen months later another of them, Bob Meder [a strong Christian], died of slow starvation. My hatred for the Japanese people nearly drove me crazy.
>
> It was soon after Meder's death that I was gripped with a strange longing to examine the Christian's Bible. I begged my

20 Philo of Alexandria, *De Agricultura Noë,* (Google Books online) § 12 (i.308); *De Somniis,* (Google Books online]), i.681, ii.25.

captors to get a Bible for me. At last, in the month of May, 1944, a guard brought the Book, but told me I could have it for only three weeks.

I eagerly began to read its pages. Chapter after chapter gripped my heart. In due time I came to the books of the prophets, and found that their every writing seemed focused on a divine Redeemer from sin, one who was to be sent from heaven to be born in the form of a human babe. Their writings so fascinated me that I read them again and again until I had earnestly studied them through six times. Then I went on into the New Testament, and there read of the birth of Jesus Christ, the one who actually fulfilled the very prophecies of Isaiah, Jeremiah, Micah and the other Old Testament writers. My heart rejoiced as I found confirmed in Acts 10:43: "To Him give all the prophets witness, that through His Name, whosoever believeth on Him shall receive remission of sins." After I had carefully read this book of the Acts, I continued on into the study of the epistle Paul wrote to the Christians at Rome.

On June 8th, 1944, the words in Romans 10:9 stood out boldly before my eyes: "If thou shalt confess with thy mouth the Lord Jesus, and shalt believe in thine heart that God hath raised Him from the dead, thou shalt be saved." In that very moment God gave me grace to confess my sins to Him, and He forgave me all my sins and saved me for Jesus' sake.[21]

After the war, Jacob went back to Japan—as a missionary. What changed Jacob DeShazer from a hater of Japanese into a lover of them? What saved his soul? The Word of God. It is truth; judge; beyond contained expression; and agent of rebirth. According to Luke 2:15, those are Jesus' functions. When the shepherds say Jesus is *rhema*, that's what it means. Put that together with John's insight and it's really clear: Jesus is

21 Jacob DeShazer, as told to Don Falkenberg. *I was a Prisoner of Japan* (Tract). Columbus, Ohio: The Bible Meditation League, 1950.

the Word. Jesus judges … is truth … belief comes through Him … and He is the agent of rebirth. That's the reality of God's Word.

RECEIVE THE WORD.

This marvelous information is not just head knowledge. It is intended to change lives. There are appropriate responses to this *rhema* "which has come to pass, which the Lord has made known. Using a tragically comedic negative example, Luke highlights the first response:

> And they [the women at the tomb to whom the angel announced Jesus' resurrection] remembered His words. Returning from the tomb, they reported all these things to the Eleven and to all the rest. Mary Magdalene, Joanna, Mary the mother of James, and the other women with them were telling the apostles these things. But these words seemed like nonsense to them, and they did not believe the women. (Luke 24:8-11 HCSB)

Our response is to receive theWord. The women received the words. They remembered. They believed. They acted on Jesus' words. They recollected and grasped the word that Jesus would rise again. The men did not. Of course, you may know that the guys got in gear later—after Jesus scared the bejeebers out of them. But the guys missed some joy and blessing because they wouldn't really incorporate God's Word into their reality. We need to receive God's Word. James 1 puts it very poetically:

> Therefore putting aside all filthiness and all that remains of wickedness, in humility receive the word implanted, which is able to save your souls. (James 1:21 NASB)

We need to receive this Word of God, to let it be implanted in our hearts. This is natural and beautiful if we'll only receive it. God has an awesome Christmas present for you. If you aren't yet a Christian, God wants you to trust Him to give you life in Jesus. If you are already a Christian, God's wants His Word planted ever more deeply in your heart. However, if a person won't receive the present, it just sits there with his or her name on the tag—unopened and un-enjoyed. Open God's gift and receive the Word.

ABIDE IN THE WORD.

Examine John's gospel and you find another response to this marvelous Word:

> So Jesus said to the Jews who had believed him, "If you abide in my word, you are truly my disciples, and you will know the truth, and the truth will set you free." (John 8:31-21 ESV)

> Abide in me, and I in you. As the branch cannot bear fruit by itself, unless it abides in the vine, neither can you, unless you abide in me. I am the vine; you are the branches. Whoever abides in me and I in him, he it is that bears much fruit, for apart from me you can do nothing. (John 15:4-5 ESV)

Abide. In what are we supposed to abide? Jesus and His word! As we learned, He is the truth. He is the one who sets hearts free. Therefore, it only makes sense that if one abides in His Word one receives all the benefits of freedom and fruitfulness. Abide means to live somewhere, to put down roots there. When former serfs from Europe came to the American frontier, they were in awe of the U.S. government's rule that anyone who would put plants—literal roots—down in the soil and abide there for five years became free and clear owner of the land. If you abide there, you become free and fruitful!

A regular question posed to me by people visiting our church is, "What's your *thing*?" Sometimes it's stated, "Whom do you follow?" Understandably, people try to get to know me as leader by discovering where I am putting down my roots. That's wise. So they ask queries like: "Are you Reformed, pastor?" "Are you an Acts 29 Networker?" "Do you follow the Willow Creek conferences?" "Are you a DTS guy?"

From the depth of my soul I always give the same response, "I am a Jesus guy!" I follow Jesus! He is the *logos* … the *rhema*. He is the one and only in whom I abide. All those other groups and leaders may be great, and I can learn from them. But God didn't give me His Word so I could be a serf to some human philosophy. God gave me Jesus so that I could abide in Him to be free and fruitful.

What about you? Are you abiding in Jesus or are you enslaved to things of earth? Even good things make you a serf unless you are abiding in Jesus.

SERVE THE WORD.

Think through this passage from Acts 6:

> "Therefore, brethren, select from among you seven men of good reputation, full of the Spirit and of wisdom, whom we may put in charge of this task. But we will devote ourselves to prayer and to the ministry of the word." (Acts 6:3-4 NASB)

In that first church in Jerusalem, the Elders are dealing with a growing set of tasks that must be accomplished in the ministry. Luke relates their solution in Acts 6. They say to the church, "Look. There's a lot of ministry to be done, and it's very important. So we're going to set aside people to get it done. But we're going to do the most critical thing—we're going to serve the word. We're going to pay attention to the Bible as Jesus' revelation."

Now examine the 25th verse of Colossians 1 written by the Apostle Paul:

> Of *this church* I was made a minister according to the stewardship from God bestowed on me for your benefit, so that I might fully carry out the *preaching of* the word of God (Colossians 1:25 NASB)

The Apostle Paul says that by God's power, he fulfills the Word of God. There is a pattern here. People who are serious about Jesus serve God's Word. That means they devote themselves to it and fulfill what it tells them. Other things matter, but serving God's Word is primary. Fulfilling God's Word is supposed to be #1.

Are you following that pattern? In your life, what's primary? Look at your schedule, your activities, and determine what is really #1. If you aren't serving the Word of God, you're missing out, because God's Word is the thing.

And notice that in each of our passages, these Christians are not serving the Word only for themselves. Devotion to God's Word blesses the people around you. My mother is devoted to quilting. So she studies a pattern, puts pieces up on her felt wall, and creates beautiful things that bless the people around her. Likewise, if we decide to devote ourselves to the Word, people around us will be warmer and happier because of our service.

REPEAT THE WORD.

Jesus is the *rhema*. Luke tells us that Jesus is the Word! So, what's a right response to that? Receive it. Abide in it. Serve it. And repeat it. Consider Acts 11:

> And behold, at that very moment three men arrived at the house in which we were, sent to me from Caesarea. And the Spirit told me to go with them, making no distinction. These six brothers also accompanied me, and we entered the man's house. And he told us how he had seen the angel stand in his house and say, 'Send to Joppa and bring Simon who is called Peter; he will declare to you a message by which you will be saved, you and all your household.' (Acts 11:11-14 ESV)

Here's the situation: Peter doesn't really think he should be sharing the word of God with Gentiles. A strict Jew, he thinks Gentiles are icky and he doesn't really consider telling them about Jesus. But God gives Peter a vision that convinces him otherwise. Immediately after the vision, these three guys arrive at his door saying, "Please come, even though we were sent by a Gentile." God makes it clear that Peter is to go with them. He does so, and shares the word of God, repeating the gospel with boldness.

And, guess what word Luke used to depict this news Peter shared? Indeed—"message" in verse 14 is a form of *rhema*. The point is that God intends His word of Jesus to be shared even when we don't really feel like passing it on.

According to my mail, nearly every Christian agrees that this is important. It's scriptural, even critical, to repeat the word of Jesus' good news. Yet according to most Christians, this rule only applies to everyone else. "My family is different. I just can't share the gospel with them." "It doesn't really apply with the people in our neighborhood." "They'll get mad or laugh at me if I share the good news of Christmas." "I am not gifted in evangelism like Peter was." On and on we share the same excuses, *ad infinitum, ad nauseam.*

Instead of our normal cop-outs, let's stop and think. I'll bet that at some point this holiday somebody is going to ask you a meaningful question … or ask you to pray for a struggle in his or her life. Right? At that moment, you have the chance to naturally, appropriately repeat the word. Just tell them! With grace and sincerity, say something like:

> Look, I don't know everything. But I know Jesus. And He is the Word of God. He is the truth and will set you free. I'll pray for you and I look forward to walking through this with you. But you must know this—Jesus loves you, died for you, and lives for you. You need to trust Him.

By God's empowering, you can speak this truth in love. You can repeat the Word of Christmas. And if it's any encouragement, know that I am praying for you receive, abide in, serve, and repeat God's Word.

Go Tell It on the Mountain
(John Wesley Work, Jr.[22])

Go, tell it on the mountain,
over the hills and everywhere.
Go, tell it on the mountain
that Jesus Christ is born.

While shepherds kept their watching
over silent flocks by night,
behold throughout the heavens,
there shone a holy light.

Go, tell it on the mountain,
over the hills and everywhere.
Go, tell it on the mountain
that Jesus Christ is born.

22 John Wesley Work, Jr., 1905. Public domain.

The shepherds feared and trembled
when lo! above the earth
rang out the angel chorus
that hailed our Saviour's birth.

Go, tell it on the mountain,
over the hills and everywhere.
Go, tell it on the mountain
that Jesus Christ is born.

Down in a lowly manger
our humble Christ was born,
and God sent us salvation,
that blessed Christmas morn.

Go, tell it on the mountain,
over the hills and everywhere.
Go, tell it on the mountain
that Jesus Christ is born.

When I am a seeker,
I seek both night and day.
I seek the Lord to help me,
and He shows me the way.

Go, tell it on the mountain,
over the hills and everywhere.
Go, tell it on the mountain
that Jesus Christ is born.

He made me a watchman
upon the city wall,
and if I am a Christian,
I am the least of all.

Go, tell it on thc mountain,
over the hills and everywhere.
Go, tell it on the mountain
that Jesus Christ is born.

THE URGENCY OF CHRISTMAS

CHAPTER SUMMARY: The shepherds received God's Word and then sought the Savior with single-minded speed. They found mind-blowing news when they met Him, and they shared the good news with all. Thus they worked both to know Jesus and to make Him known.

LIFE CHANGE OBJECTIVE: That we are urgent and purposeful about sharing Jesus.

I WANT CHRISTMAS TO COME NOW.

My niece Rebekah is a wonderful young lady who was blessed to trust Jesus early in her life. She is a complete delight and we have enjoyed many rich conversations together about life as Christians. A few years ago when Rebekah was still a very little girl, we had a particularly striking chat. Almost as soon as I said, "Hello, Bekah Bee [her name for herself at the time], she declared, "Uncle Wayne, I wrote a song for you about Christmas." And employing a tune she made up, Rebekah sang these lyrics:

I'm ready for Christmas now.
I'm ready for Christmas to come.
I want it to come now.
I want Christmas to come NOW!

As you can imagine, that blessed me—and not just because my niece is so precious. Her song appealed to me because I think it captures how people felt in the first century. There was deep longing—a longing of which one can hear an echo in the song we sing at Christmas, "O Come, O Come, Emmanuel."

O come, O come, Emmanuel,
And ransom captive Israel,
That mourns in lonely exile here
Until the Son of God appear.
Rejoice! Rejoice! Emmanuel
shall come to thee, O Israel.

O come, Thou Rod of Jesse, free
Thine own from Satan's tyranny;
From depths of hell Thy people save,
And give them victory over the grave.
Rejoice! Rejoice! Emmanuel
shall come to thee, O Israel.

O come, Thou Day-spring, come and cheer
Our spirits by Thine advent here;
And drive away the shades of night
And pierce the clouds and bring us light!
Rejoice! Rejoice! Emmanuel
shall come to thee, O Israel.[23]

23 Latin text "Veni, veni, Emmanuel" translated to English by John Mason Neale and Henry Sloane Coffin. 1850s. Public domain.

URGENCY TO KNOW HIM AND MAKE HIM KNOWN

There was a heady expectation 2000 years ago. People were longing for salvation. They were eagerly awaiting the first Christmas, if you will. People were ready for Christ—the Messiah—to come, which explains the shepherds' response we've been studying in this book. When confronted with the great news of Christmas, they responded like this:

> So they came in a hurry and found their way to Mary and Joseph, and the baby as He lay in the manger. When they had seen this, they made known the statement which had been told them about this Child. And all who heard it wondered at the things which were told them by the shepherds. (Luke 2:16-18 NASB)

Remember, the shepherds have just had an angel of God appear to them. The angel was backed up by a huge heavenly army declaring God's glory. And God said through the angel that the Messiah had come! He told the shepherds to go to Bethlehem and find the baby who was born as the Christ, the Savior. Consider their reaction to all this:

- These shepherds received God's Word.
- They sought the Savior with single-minded speed.
- They shared the good news with others.

In summary, they worked both to know Jesus and to make Him known. In their response the shepherds teach us how to respond to the urgency of Christmas.

Speudo

There are three important terms in Luke 2:16-18—special words that teach us how to respond to the urgent need of a Savior. The terms are "in a hurry," "found," and "made known." These words provide a powerful, life-changing pattern for us to follow.

"In a hurry" is the Greek term *speusantes* [σπεύσαντες], an adverb of strong activity. It means to fly after something. The root word is *speudo* [σπεύδω, pronounced "spew dough."] I taught this term once and a teenager said it reminded him of the time his sister made cookies and forgot the sugar. "We spewed dough for sure!" he said.

That's a pretty good picture! It races … it flies out of your mouth. Of course, the name *speudo* also resembles a famous racing swimsuit company. If you ever swam competitively you likely had to wear a Speedo bathing suit. They were designed to make you go fast. Speedo was built for speed. (It certainly wasn't for fashion!) In that sense, Speedo is like *speudo*.

In haste—*speudo*—the shepherds ran as quickly as possible. They ran like a five year-old going to the tree on Christmas morning. Why? Because they recognize the import of Jesus. They realize how badly they need a Savior. They are in need and thus they want Christmas to come NOW!

We are in the same spot. We need our Savior. We need Christmas NOW! Therefore, if we are wise, we move toward Jesus in a hurry. *Speudo*.

Aneurysko

Luke suggests that the shepherds had to search for Jesus; that they had to find their way to Him in Bethlehem. And that's our second critical term: found. It's the Greek *aneuran* [ἀνεῦραν], a word that appears only in Luke in the Bible. *Aneuran* is a form of a medical term *aneurysko* [ἀνευρίσκω], which was used of an internal explosion in the brain. Of course, we still use this term in English today, referring to a balloon-like bulge of a vessel inside the brain as an "aneurysm."

Luke was a doctor, but why would he use *this* word for "found?" One reason is obviously that *aneuran* means to "find after searching diligently." God wants us to know that the shepherds really looked for Jesus; after all, the family was staying with the animals that night. But another reason is likely found in the medical aspect of *aneurysko*. Doctors really search hard for aneurysms because they are so transformative. Luke could be telling us that the shepherds found mind-blowing news in that stable. This was really the Savior of the world. This was the Messiah promised and prophesied. This was explosive. This would change the thinking of the world forever. The shepherds were in haste [*pseudo*] and what they found in Jesus was mind-blowing [*aneurysko*.]

Ginosko

Now, let's examine the third word, this time reading Luke's report in a different English translation:

> And when they had seen *it*, they made known abroad the saying which was told them concerning this child. And all they that heard *it* wondered at those things which were told them by the shepherds. (Luke 2:17-18 KJV)

Just as they were urgent to meet Jesus, these men were equally purposeful in sharing the reality of the Savior with others. I love the old KJV here, as "made known abroad" captures the breadth and depth of the Greek word *egnorisan* [ἐγνώρισαν]. It means to diligently present knowledge and is derived from the primitive Greek root *ginosko* [γινώσκω]—an early term for knowing something.

Ginosko is a very particular word chosen by God for His author Luke to use. It is somewhat like *contaron* in Spanish. Usually translated "recounted," *contaron* is from the Latin compound *computo* or *conputo* meaning "with reckoning." Thus, there is a depth of computation, of understanding, involved in *contaron*. That's why all three Spanish translations I own render *egnorisan* (the English "made known abroad") as *contaron*. The Spanish translators chose *contaron* in order to highlight the depth of understanding in the shepherds. You can't share what you don't really think through and own. As the Romans might have said, otherwise it doesn't "compute."

Like *computo* and *contaron*, *ginosko* stands out among all the possible words for knowing because *ginosko* means depth of thought and understanding. These shepherds *ginosko*. Thus, they can make Jesus known [*egnorisan*] with depth and understanding. It is their internal relationship to truth that empowers their external sharing.

Egnorisan also carries one final thought—urgency. That's why the KJV added "abroad" to "made known." The shepherds felt the urgency of Christmas not just in finding but also in sharing. They made known what they had come to know: the mind-blowing news that Jesus is the Messiah.

Compute

Think this through as we prepare for Christmas. Some of us enjoy Christmas for the tradition, and that is wonderful. But sadly that tradition can morph into complacent traditionalism. We must break the icy coating of rote traditionalism off of our traditions. Otherwise, we will become rigid and self-focused, losing the urgency of Christmas. Think! Remember! What all people need has happened. The Messiah has come. We must reckon on that again. We must fly to Jesus, enjoy afresh the mind-blowing truth revealed only in Him, and then share what we know. That's what Luke was saying in those word choices.

Of course, one must know Jesus in order to share about Him. This where the non-Christian tenses up and says to himself, "Uh, Oh! Here is comes. This is the part where that preacher tries to save my soul." Yep. You're right. Well, partially right. Actually, it's not me wanting to save your soul. It's God. God is the one who sent His Son to earth in order to save you. Jesus is the One who sacrificed his life for you and rose from the dead so that by trusting Him your soul could be saved from Hell. Messiah Jesus is a mind-blowing gift. He offers you heaven. So this urgency of Christmas is between you and God.

I will add this little foreshadowing about your conversation with God: You're going to lose. Jesus said that you will lose. That loss occurs in one of two ways.

1. You can surrender your rebellious desire to be your own God and thereby find life forever in the Messiah. As Jesus promised:

   Whoever loses his life for my sake will find it. (Matthew 10:39b ESV)

2. You can keep fighting against God and lose your soul forever. Jesus commented on this in the same breath:

   Whoever finds his life will lose it, and whoever loses his life for my sake will find it. (Matthew 10:39 ESV)

See? You will lose either way. In option one, you lose only what humans absurdly call "life"—a combination of rebellion, sin, and selfish pride. For Jesus' sake, that trust in a flawed self is traded for trust in the perfect Christ. In option two, you lose the chance to enjoy God forever. Given those binary choices, I encourage you to trust Jesus as your Savior. Because there is loss either way, you might as well receive God's Christmas present of real life. That way, your "loss" of pride actually becomes your gain of finding everlasting life.

Now, for Christians, there is urgency as well. We are secure in our salvation in Jesus. But there is an entire world that needs to hear about the fact that Messiah has come! So, you and I need to feel a sense of urgency. I pray that we recommit to being God's shepherds who go in haste to share what we know: the mind-blowing news of Jesus the Christ who has brought true joy to the world.

Joy to the World

(Isaac Watts [24])

Joy to the world! the Lord is come;
Let earth receive her King;
Let every heart prepare him room,
And heaven and nature sing,
And heaven and nature sing,
And heaven, and heaven, and nature sing.

Joy to the world! the Saviour reigns;
Let men their songs employ;
While fields and floods, rocks, hills, and plains
Repeat the sounding joy,
Repeat the sounding joy,
Repeat, repeat the sounding joy.

No more let sins and sorrows grow,
Nor thorns infest the ground;
He comes to make His blessings flow
Far as the curse is found,
Far as the curse is found,
Far as, far as, the curse is found.

24 Isaac Watts. 1719. Public domain.

He rules the world with truth and grace,
And makes the nations prove
The glories of His righteousness,
And wonders of His love,
And wonders of His love,
And wonders, wonders, of His love.

A FINAL THOUGHT

I was blessed to discuss this book with Dr. Tim Demy—a gifted professor, leader, and fellow fan of Luke's writing. After reading this manuscript, Tim wrote me a note that I feel captures the point of our study:

> Wayne, I enjoyed this look at the first Christmas—Luke's curious Christmas. And indeed, it was a curious, remarkable, and miraculous one! In the wonderful Charles Dickens story *A Christmas Carol,* one engages with the imaginary Ghost of Christmas Past, Ghost of Christmas Present, and Ghost of Christmas Future. Those were fictional. What Luke presented is not. What he relates through his remarkable gospel given under the authority and inspiration of God the Holy Spirit is the story of the Christ of Christmas past, the Christ of Christmas present, and the Christ of Christmas future. Indeed, Scripture tells us that Jesus Christ is the Eternal Son of God.

Amen! Tim is correct. Jesus is the Savior of the world who through his birth, death, burial, and resurrection brings eternal life to all who believe. I pray that you trust Him as Savior. Then this Christmas and every one to come will be blessed beyond measure.

ADVENT SUGGESTIONS

Thank you for the privilege of walking together through this adventure. If you are looking to further emphasize Jesus' Christmas word-power, the following suggestions may prove useful.

Church: Don't let the busyness of the holidays keep you from church. Attend with your whole soul engaged. Let the familiar stories ring true and new to your heart. Use your mind to think through the emphases God has put on the heart of your pastor. Take notes. Pray. Listen. If you find yourself without a church home, prayerfully begin the process of joining one. Ask God to guide you to a place where the Bible is the supreme authority and where you can give yourself to redeemed community.

Neighborhood: Look for opportunities to talk with your neighbors about the issues raised by Luke. I am always blessed by how even dedicated atheists enjoy talking about words and what they mean. Share a copy of this book and you'll likely find they will read it. Especially invite your neighbors to church. On Christmas Eve we find many neighbors are interested in going to church with us. You may discover the same is true where you live, but you will only find out if you ask.

Home: In our home we light advent candles every year, continuing a tradition begun by our Reformed forbears from Germany. There are many great guides available for you in this activity. Here's one twist that may help drive home what we've studied together: name the candles for each of Luke's big topics. Thus, the candles become the candles of Joy and Peace, Humility, the Word, Urgency, and the Savior of Christmas.

Although we celebrate Advent and Christmas for a few weeks each year, we should never forget that we have the opportunity to celebrate Jesus Christ—the Christ of Christmas and Savior of the world every day of the year!

ACKNOWLEDGEMENTS

Thanks to Lampion Press for their passion for this book and the ATD series, and special kudos to Tim for more magnificent editing and to Amy for great cover design and formatting. Thanks also to Carolyn Powell for excellent proof-reading.

The All The Difference board chose this title from our possible candidates. Thanks to them for that and for their supportive guidance in everything. Thank you, Ricky, Tracey, Paul, Toni, Eric, Shannon, Margi, Tom, Rich, and Roland.

Finally and most significantly, my sweetheart Janna navigated me through this work with amazing grace and wisdom. I am richly blessed to labor alongside her and our children Jessica, Michael, and Benjamin.

ABOUT THE AUTHOR

Wayne Braudrick serves as Senior Pastor of Frisco Bible Church in Frisco, Texas. He also teaches on many radio stations through the *All the Difference* daily broadcast and serves as adjunct faculty for Ouachita Baptist University. Dr. Braudrick earned his doctorate in leadership communication through Middlesex University in London; gained a master's degree in Bible at Dallas Theological Seminary; and was a National Merit Scholar at Baylor University where he read history, literature, and education. Wayne lives with his marvelous family in Frisco, Texas, where he and his wife refuse to let work come in the way of their regular racquetball games.

ALSO AVAILABLE BY WAYNE BRAUDRICK:

Whatever Happened to Manhood?
A Return to Biblical Manhood

Whatever Happened to Manhood?
A Return to Biblical Manhood
Study Guide